LABORATORY EAST
École Polytechnique Fédérale de Lausanne

Plans & Images
—— An Archive of Projects on Typology in Architecture 2013–2018

Edited by
Martin Fröhlich
Anja Fröhlich
Tiago P. Borges
Sebastian F. Lippok

PARK BOOKS

Introduction: On Lit avec les Yeux

Tiago P. Borges

<u>How to read a plan</u>

In his text "Lire: esquisse socio-physiologique", first published in the magazine *Esprit* in 1976 and later reissued in the compilation *Penser/Classer*, Georges Perec talks about the act of reading. In it, the writer structures a set of notes on what he calls the "economy of reading", focusing on different characteristics of this endeavour. Perec's choice of words to describe reading is fortuitous, and, as is commonly accepted, fortuitousness comes only by dint of hard work: "Reading is an act", he states. "We must try to grasp not the message received, but the receiving of the message at an elementary level, that is to say: What happens when you read. Eyes alight on lines and move about, but many other things accompany the movement.... You don't just read anyhow, any time, any place, even if you read just anything."[1]

What Perec seems to be suggesting is that the process of reading and all of its constraints are more important that the "object" one reads. But is this reasoning contrary to other readings? Does reading architecture, or for that matter reading a working drawing – which is a codified representation of a building – obey identical protocols? Above all, do Perec's connotations also have a resonance for this other nature of reading? In answer, he would have us believe "there could be an art of reading – and not just of reading written text, but also of what is called the reading of a painting, or a city – based on reading obliquely, on looking at the text from a different angle."[2] I personally am convinced that it is precisely this "reading obliquely" ("*un regard oblique*") that is specific to the act of reading architecture, and that this in turn is also what – thankfully – makes any attempt to normalise that act difficult. In essence, if we have different ways of reading the same identical codes, how can we be sure of understanding the same message? Are these differences dangerous or advantageous? What is the influence of one's accumulated visual background, and how can this factor be measured above that of the act of reading?

On the one hand, architecture on paper follows clearly established representational conventions that are subject to the rules of geometry, which for various reasons and at a certain point can and should be questioned. These conventions as usually difficult to tackle – a line is to be seen as a limit and a texture usually indicates matter. On the other hand, there is less unanimity in speaking about the conventions of reading. There is no universal protocol on how to read an architectural drawing. To read (architecture) is a free act – certainly informed by conventions, but never restricted by them. One can read the voids, the paper surface untouched by the plotter's ink, or one can read the lines, its thickness, that delimit the spaces later to be built. If the outcome is potentially still similar, the narrative of that act of reading is nevertheless as unique as the reader. The movement of the trained eye will tend to vary, as much as fluctuations in its speed will too, the eye having the tendency to read faster what is more easily apprehensible and to freeze to carefully analyse a more demanding detail. This can lie either in the complexity of the representation or in the richness of the interpretation. It is difficult to find a more apposite description of what the indefatigable Georges Perec calls the *regard oblique* than in his remark, "Eyes do not read letters one after the other, nor so they read whole words one after the other, nor lines after the other, but proceed in spurts and stops, exploring simultaneously the whole visual field of reading with dogged redundancy: ceaseless movements punctuated by minute halts, as if in order to find what is sought, the eye had to sweep the page with intense agitation [...] in an aleatory, muddled and repetitive fashion [...] like a pigeon pecking the ground as it hunts for breadcrumbs."[3]

How to read an archive

Along with the growing (re-)appreciation of the architecture drawing as a medium, the archives of architectural practices are likely to assume a new mediational dimension. Architecture archives have the potential to become new museums of architecture, and they will undoubtedly serve as prime vehicles in the narratives to come. In this respect, there are two essential aspects to consider: firstly, the archive as a repository of architectural representations – from sketches and collages to working drawings and models – which ensures their preservation and grows chronologically; and, secondly, the archive as a reading room where one can trace not only the guiding threads of an architectural project and ancillary research records, but also the "*catalogue raisonée*" of a practice.[4] This second facet constitutes the archive in is its more ambitious configuration. In both scenarios, the archive will always remain at the whim of the choices or the discipline of its "builder", the balance between what is kept and what discarded – which is a project in itself. The assemblage of an archive can be non-linear, swayed either by the *modus operandi* of its author or by the temporality of its constitutive elements. Proportional to the importance of an archive of architecture is its operable value: it is its "operability" that prevents it from becoming a mere database, a pinboard storefront or a showcase portfolio. This operability can either be historical, when the archive is the matter of *a posteriori* studies; or it can be project-related, either for the maker or for others, when the archive constitutes the architect's drawing table. Beyond the mere accumulation of documents, the archive then becomes an accumulation of knowledge. This other kind of archive calls for obsessive practice and a keen awareness of a "design-through-research" approach. Inside an operative architecture archive, each project is not an end in itself, rather the end has no end – or to express it otherwise, the archive is a locus of open ends. Each project potentially contains the seed of the next, or alternatively may itself simply become a new project responding to new external constraints.[5] In his essay "An Archival Impulse", Hal Foster describes the archive as the place of "unfulfilled beginnings or incomplete projects – in art and in history alike – that might offer points of departure again."[6] The operative archive develops – still quoting Foster – "through mutations of connections and disconnections".[7]

It is the archive's role to house the raw universe of each project, namely everything that transcends the physical limitations of a press release or a published monograph. Accessing an operative archive is to access an "alternative knowledge"[8] and to recognise the archive's incompleteness. It is a toolbox that challenges us to accept Perec's lesson about reading obliquely in order to extract "signifying elements", just like birds eagerly looking for "meaning-crumbs".[9]

An archive for reading obliquely

The intersection between the two ideas – Georges Perec's argument for "reading obliquely" and the archive as an operational entity that can inform and transform an architectural project – moulds the framework of this current book. Concretely, by rejecting the static condition of printed matter, the reader's operative use of the pages that follow will hopefully make these two hypotheses evident.

In this sense, this publication is not intended to be an exhaustive report. Instead, this compilation of the outcome of the first few years of the Laboratory of Elementary Architecture and Studies of Types (EAST), at École Polytechnique Fédérale de Lausanne, from 2013 to 2018, is something more akin to a large contact sheet: a selection of third-year students' projects that, assembled in book form, enables an identification and decipherment of the core research developed at the design studio.

At design studio EAST, students are required to challenge architectural typologies, first of all by reading and redrawing – essential tasks in order to be able to understand a programme, clarify its relations and identify types. Students explore key reference projects to determine constant characteristics. After this core exercise, they decompose and recompose each element of the programme with the aim of injecting new dynamics into it. One of the goals of their projects is to test new hybrid types – a kind of architectural graftage capable of responding to contemporary demands. Finally, in dissolving a project, the students are encouraged to identify its central element, namely the room as a basic unit, and to work on its formal properties or its pictorial qualities – both of these researches feature here in the section "The Best Room". These references later inform the full-scale projects that are also documented in the colour pages of this book. From large-scale projects with a strong urban component to small-scale rooms, from urban textures to construction details, the pavilions that were ultimately built and are presented here emulate all the richness of architecture, regardless of the shift of scale proposed during each one-year term. These 1:1 projects are also the result of external collaborations that inscribe the remit of each project into a real-life situation and anticipate the one-year internship ahead of each student.

To print this archive also required some editorial choices. Each project is represented only by two elements: one image and one drawing. This deliberate and radical economy of means tests each project's capacity to communicate its central intention, and requires a willingness of readers to switch between plans and images. Equipped with its pedagogical and academic fulcrums, this publication can be regarded as a source book in that it deals with a variety of architectural issues and the multiple ways of representing them. Far from being addressed uniformly, these questions are explored by means of collage and renderings, but also through paintings, images of cast plaster volumes and photographs of cardboard models. In this process, the essential thought is that the construction of a space and the construction of the image that represents it are of equally critical importance. With its key emphasis on the visual, *Plans & Images: An Archive of Projects on Typology in Architecture* is an invitation to look, to look again, and to look even closer again. Just like Perec's birds.

---

1 "Reading", in Georges Perec, *Thoughts of Sorts*, trans. David Bellos (Boston, MA: David R. Godine, 2009), pp. 87–102, here p. 88–89.

2 Ibid. p. 92: "Un certain art de la lecture – et pas seulement la lecture d'un texte, mais ce que l'on appelle la lecture d'un tableau, ou la lecture d'une ville – pourrait consister à lire de côté, à porter sur le texte un regard oblique?"

3 Ibid. p. 90.

4 Kent Kleinman also discusses this aspect, arguing that the archive is less "a record of the genesis of a built or projected work as it is a supplement for the qualities that the built work will inevitably lack." However, the opposite is also likely to occur when a built project offers what its multiple representations never reveal. See Kent Kleinman, "Archiving/Architecture", *Archival Science*, 1 (2001), pp. 321–32.

5 One example of this would be the manner in which OMA's single-family house Y2K evolves to become the Casa da Música project in Porto, certainly transcending what Rem Koolhaas ironically described as "naked opportunism".
Another would be how the research undertaken by a resilient practice such as Lacaton & Vassal – and in this case it is the office's core element – is continuously exploited, reworked and refined.

6 Hal Foster, "An Archival Impulse" *October*, 110 (Fall 2004), pp. 3–22, here p. 5.

7 Ibid, p. 6.

8 Ibid.

9 Perec, *Thoughts*, p. 90.

Contents

5
Tiago P. Borges:
On Lit avec les Yeux

24 — 97
Private City

12 — 23
Best Room Pavilion

98 — 143
The Best Home

26
Anja Fröhlich:
Ownership and
Urban Fabric

84
Klaus-Dieter Weiß:
Delimiting Dwelling: The House,
the Apartment and the City

100
Tiago P. Borges:
The Best Home for All

138
Antje Bittorf:
Supermarket, Superhome

156 — 287
The Best Room

158
Anja Fröhlich and
Martin Fröhlich:
Good, Better, the Best

234
Anja Fröhlich and
Martin Fröhlich:
The Art of Seeing

284
Marie Theres Stauffer:
A Brief History
of the Living Room

Laboratory EAST

Contents

144 — 155
Cabanon Art Pavilion

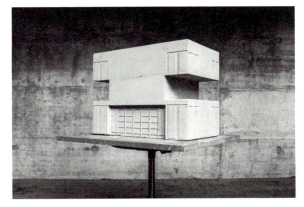

288 — 299
A Neuve Twin Pavilions

300 — 355
Modern Times

356 — 407
Steal Schinkel

358
Anja Fröhlich and Martin Fröhlich: Towards a New Bauakademie

402
Roland Züger: Urban Design as Constellation

408 — 419
Traverse Art Pavilion

302
Tiago P. Borges: The Pursuit of Happiness

336
Rafael Moneo: On Typology

352
Interview: Rafael Moneo

421 — 432
About Editors, Authors,
Partners & Students

430 — 431
Credits & Colophon

What makes a room "the best room"? This question was taken as both a motto and a guideline. Hundreds of thoughts, drawings, models and mock-ups were produced until each element attained its needed equilibrium within the greater ensemble. Here, at the crossroads between space, construction and atmosphere, the project emerged. External variants, such as building costs, administrative procedures, local legislation — and even bad weather — played a role, but each constraint was embraced not as a hindrance but as a potential enrichment. Despite its temporary nature, upon conclusion the Best Room pavilion served as a new cultural heart of the EPFL campus.

Best Room Pavilion

Photographs
Joël Tettamanti

2015

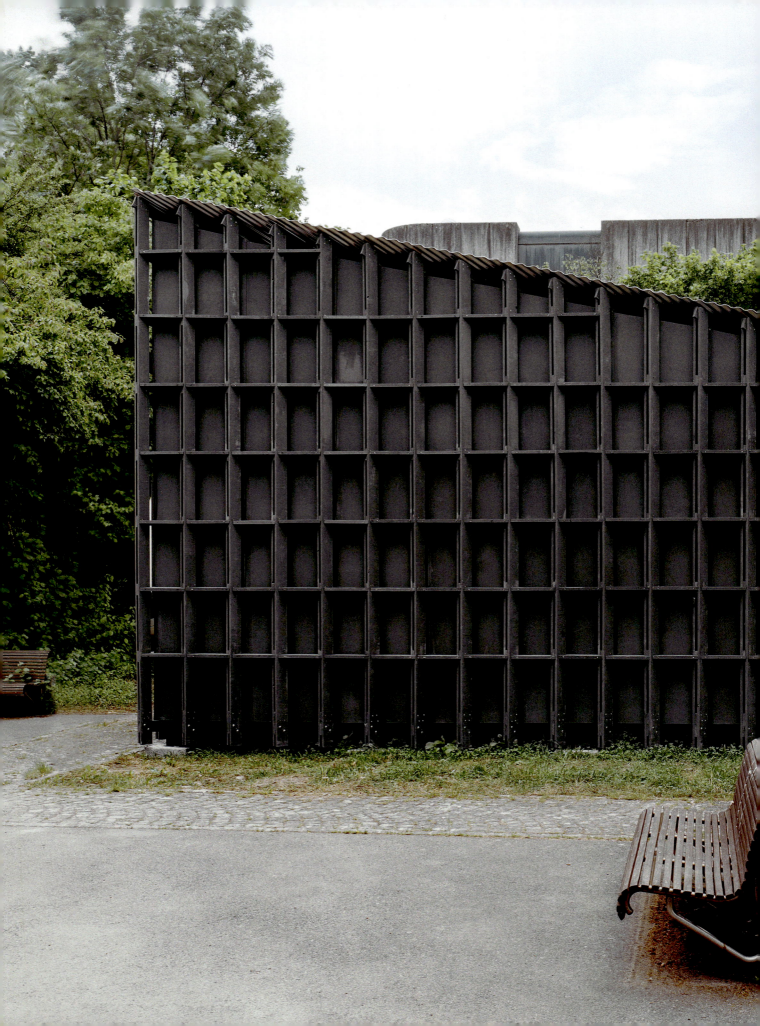

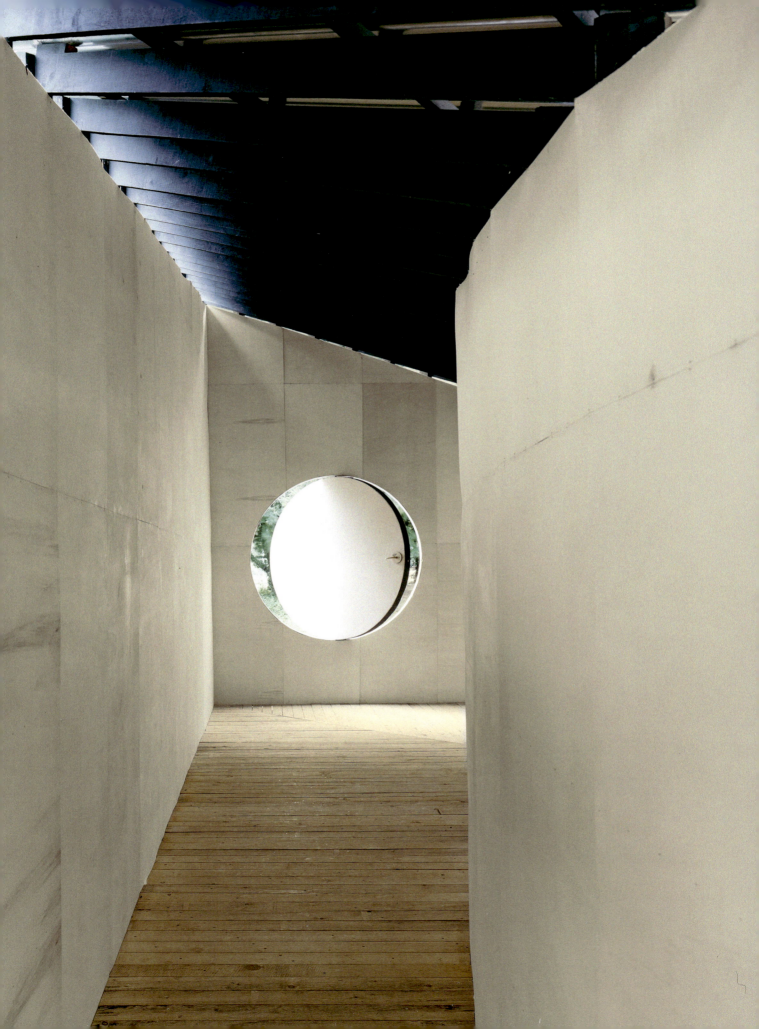

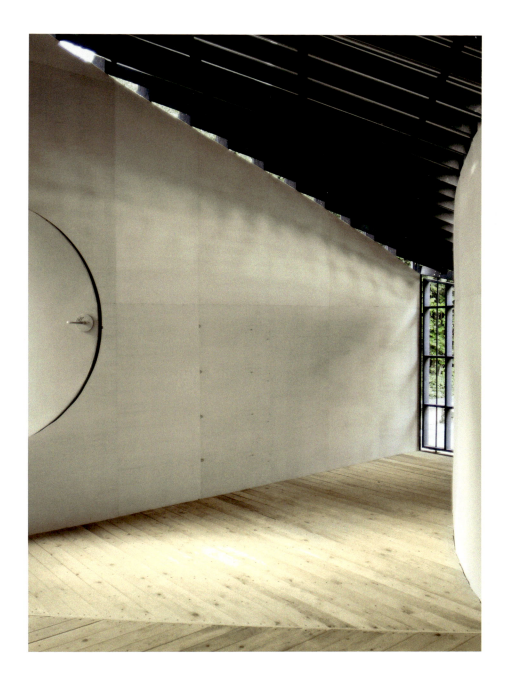

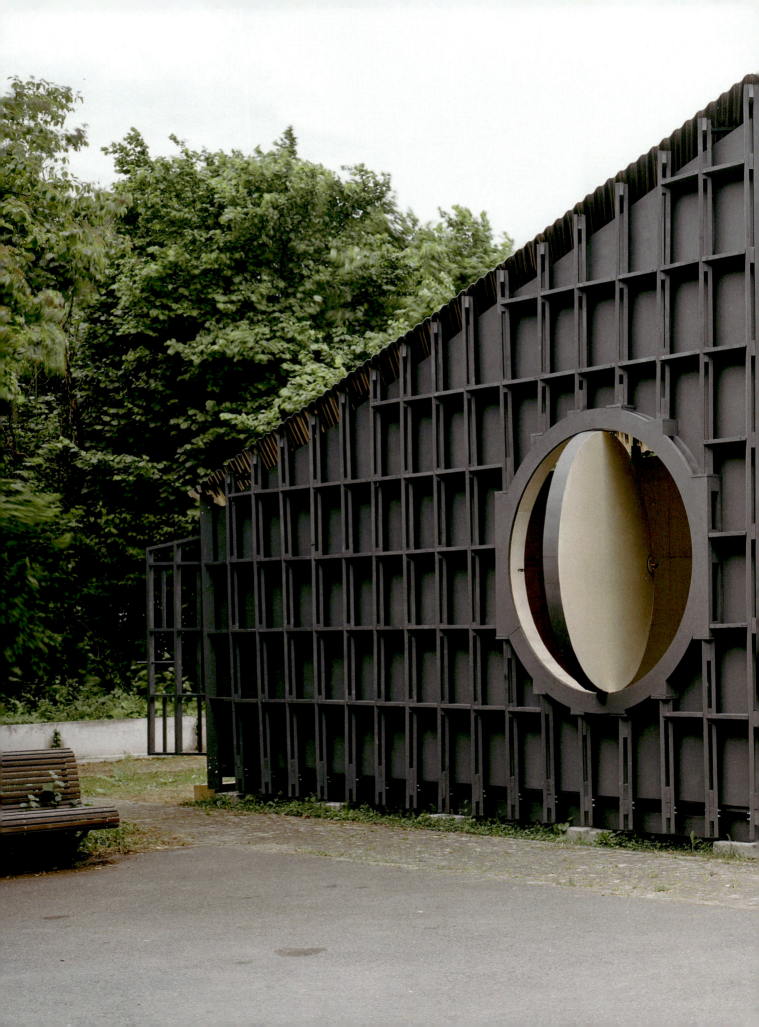

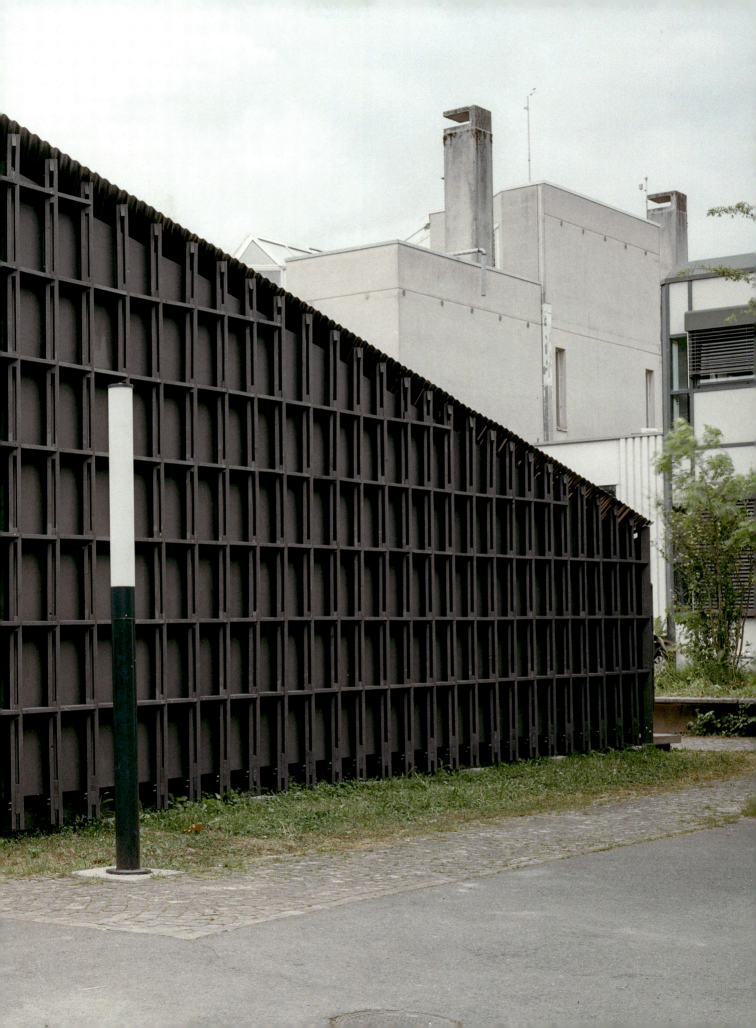

Chapter 1

2013

Private City

Based on the results of an urban-design competition for two different sites — in Renens and Berlin — the students were asked to design a multi-family residence within the fictional framework of a self-build initiative involving a group purchasing and developing a plot of land together for themselves. The goal was to create different living qualities and typologies based on the interrelationships between public and private property. The underlying core question was to what extent does private property ownership affect the urbanity of a given context without diluting essential public claims to overall urban culture?

If one considers that private land ownership and the quality of public spaces of the city are interrelated, to what extent can the first be used as an instrument to secure communal, public space in our cities?

Ownership and Urban Fabric

Anja Fröhlich

Every age has its own vision of living in the city. These ideas are often manifested most clearly when the land on which a new quarter or settlement is built belongs to a single landowner. This can be seen, for example, in the military colonies from Roman times or the founding of cities in the Middle Ages, where private ownership of individual plots of land was all but impossible. Other urban settlement forms, such as garden cities, make the fundamental role that the ownership of the land plays particularly apparent. The fact that the ground on which they were built was common land, owned either by the municipality or a cooperative, meant that the resulting buildings were usually designed according to a coordinated plan. Conversely, where land is divided into many individually owned plots, people tend to build according to their own wishes, with correspondingly heterogeneous results.

Today, the land on which the city is built and into which it expands belongs to a great many individual owners. To be able to influence the kind and size of buildings, the city uses laws and regulations in an attempt to ensure that new quarters are interwoven into the fabric of the city.

The mission of the design studio was to create a residential quarter composed of individual projects.

Using the means of land parcelling, the positioning of the building on the plot and the number of storeys and materials, the goal was to achieve an appropriate degree of shared identity, closure and homogeneity within the quarter. A central challenge was to find a balance between the public need for urban community and the private interests and personal tastes of the respective landowners.

The idea of creating housing in the city also responds to the current architectural debate on increasing the density of cities. Here, the focus of design narrows down successively from the public realm, which defines the structure of the quarter, to the typologies of buildings and forms of living within it, and to the articulation of the facades; in other words, from the structural system to its atmospheric impression.

A number of different scenarios are conceivable in this context: for example, infill projects for vacant plots, interventions in and the renewal of existing structures, or the design of entire urban districts. As a counter-tendency to the building of single-family houses, urban housing brings with it the potential to create identity. In this sense, housing, coupled with its public and private areas, has become a key instrument of urban architecture. As concrete examples, the projects explored the new phenomenon of urban density by investigating two quarters selected for their urban-development potential.

1 – The Urban Neighbourhood

The Urban Neighbourhood project investigated the strategy of urban intervention as a means of effecting urban renewal and increasing density in inner cities. In terms of design proposals, it provided an opportunity to compare the qualities of two specific urban residential neighbourhoods: the La Savonnerie site in Renens near Lausanne and the Freudenberg site in the Friedrichshain district of Berlin.

The design deliberations needed, on the one hand, to consider abstract aspects, such as the urban grammar, and to analyse the structural and typological manifestations of urban architecture in all its morphological variations. At the same time, a vision for the concrete visual and atmospheric dimension of urban space needed to be elaborated that encompassed both its private and its communal qualities.

This goal of creating a new distinctive urban environment involved analysing not only the site itself but also its relationship to the existing urban structure of the surroundings, culminating in an urban-design proposal similar to a master plan for the respective quarter.

The spatial structure of the master plans had to then be broken down into individual plots of land. A plot is a robust unit that orders the urban fabric and should also accommodate the needs of generations to come. Through possession of a plot of land, the owner is bound to the land and has a share in the city. Their right to ownership confers them the freedom to build as they wish within certain predefined parameters and regulations. The master plan must therefore lay down a set of rules that outline how individual plots of land relate to the quarter as a whole.

In the design project, the object was to investigate how the size and structure of land parcels influence the resulting building typologies and the characteristics of the quarter, especially with respect to the relationship between private land ownership and communal uses. To what extent can private land ownership be used as an instrument to secure communal, public space in our cities? To what degree does private ownership influence the public qualities of the city?

Renens – La Savonnerie site

Located outside the city centre of Lausanne, this quarter is situated in a predominantly mixed, semi-urban context. Originally a constellation of dispersed individual buildings with a blend of housing and commercial uses, the district was to be transformed into a principally residential inner-city neighbourhood.

The design projects therefore addressed issues such as the density, concentration and urban consolidation and autonomy of the new quarter. The resulting underlying urban fabric took the form of a spatial continuum with a succession of different urban spaces and hierarchies. Peaceful garden courtyards lie on the private sides of the urban blocks, which are composed of individual apartment buildings. Inserted like implants into the heterogeneous structure of their urban surroundings, the projects give the quarter a special character.

Berlin – Freudenberg site

A new quarter was to be planned on the site of the former Freudenberg production works in Friedrichshain in Berlin. The objective of the design project for one of the few remaining inner-city sites in the heart of the Wilhelmine quarter was to convert it into much-needed housing, complemented by spacious public green areas and parks. Landscape architecture was to play a key role in the concept.

Drawing inspiration from historical block forms, the proposed projects fan out in calm, orderly arrangements of apartment buildings around one or more central squares, creating a harmonious urban panorama. The dominant typology is that of a large block with a courtyard, garden and terraces. On the one hand, the projects strive to continue the structure of the historical context, while, on the other, ensuring that they retain an autonomy of their own through the formal language of their architecture.

2 – Neighbourhood housing

The planning of a new urban quarter generally begins with the question of a master plan that sets out the design parameters determining the general framework for the individual residential buildings. In this exercise, the framework attempted to find a balance between permitting architectural variety in the details while achieving a sense of general coherence and continuity. It set out clear rules for the size and positioning of the specific building volumes that served as design parameters for the subsequent design of quite different house types, in turn resulting in an urban district that is both compact and distinctive.

The Urban Neighbourhood projects for the Renens La Savonnerie site and the Berlin Freudenberg site were analysed and two master plans selected for the next stage, consisting of the development of individual apartment buildings as part of a larger group of buildings. The objective was to encourage different living qualities and housing typologies – in terms of the relationship between public space and private property – to exist alongside one another within the stipulations of the master plan.

The spectrum of the design task ranged from the smallest unit, the private dwelling, to the design of public communal areas that act as more than mere functional circulation spaces. Simultaneously, the projects also examined the possibility of incorporating generally usable shared areas into the housing floor plans, for example by relocating selected private functions into communally used spaces.

In this sense, this is a response to the idea that contemporary forms of housing should ideally also try to fuse the benefits of the single-family house with those of apartment living. In addition to examining interactions between neighbours within the building, the design projects also had to consider how they respond to or influence the buildings on the neighbouring plots, for example concerning the placement of windows and firewalls.

With respect to realm the question of how private land ownership can be used as an instrument to secure communal space in the public realm, the projects also needed to consider the typology of private realms in the city, and in particular the typology of the apartment as the smallest unit within the neutral container of the city. The design of the individual apartment buildings needed to find a balance between developing a general progression of spaces and accommodating individual variation. In addition to affording typological variance, key aspects of the design problem included defining core areas for services and circulation as well as clear perimeter boundaries.

Renens – La Savonnerie site

Stipulated within the master plan was a linear succession of individual buildings defined by a rigid grid starting at the edges of the block. The radical rigorousness of the block patchwork produced an especially distinctive urban structure – a compact, dense urban fabric with clear street spaces, almost medieval in character, but also attractive private spaces for the residents.

The design projects placed strong emphasis on a sense of unity and identity within the new urban quarter while also presenting numerous variations on the typology of the freestanding urban villa. A continuous plinth provided a common datum line for the individual, separately rendered buildings, anchoring them and emphasising the level of the pavement. With a prescribed height of four to five storeys and a shop zone on the ground floor, a range of quite different housing typologies was developed.

Berlin – Freudenberg site

The master plan adopted the typical Berlin pattern of firewall construction, creating a clear urban structure of apartment buildings, with the building formations varying where they meet at the firewall.

At the same time, the master plan positioned freestanding urban apartment buildings along the block perimeter, separated by narrow slots. Similarly, the design stipulations of the master plan also produced urban frontages with tall window formats and loggias or terraces. This served as a design framework for the articulation of the individual buildings, which surround a communal courtyard and/or garden. The overall structure is an elementary constellation of urban architecture comprising road, block, building and courtyard garden.

A characteristic of all the projects was the different individual building forms that nevertheless adhered to the building typology of the quarter. Floor plans were developed in response to the respective form of the apartment building, and interpreted it inwards. All the floor plans had a large hallway, some with two-storey open gallery spaces. In almost all the floor plans, the sleeping areas were segregated from the living areas. Spacious loggias allowed the private realm to spill outwards and, in most cases, afforded a direct view of the green areas within the block interior.

Scale 1:200

Alyssa Antonuccio

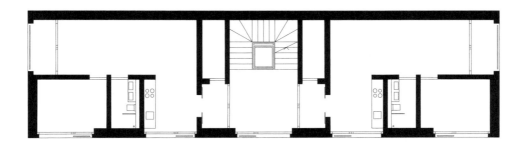

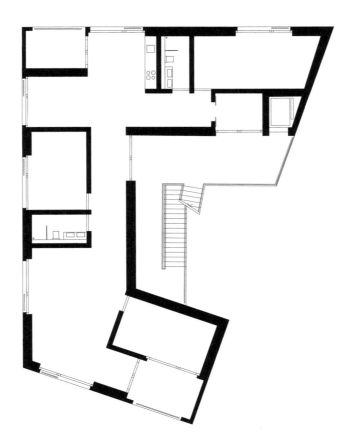

Laboratory EAST   Private City

Arnaud Baudouin

Scale 1:200

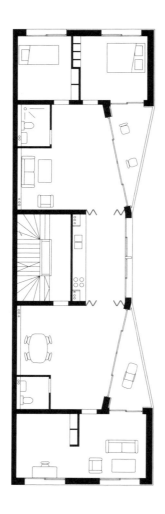
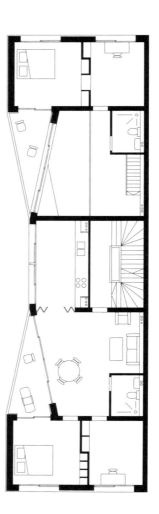

Private City · Laboratory EAST

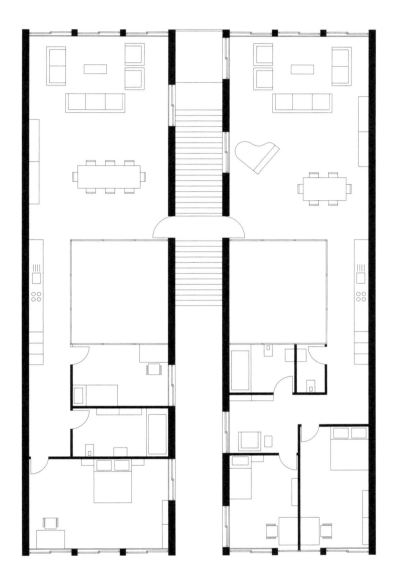

Adrien Comte

Scale 1:200

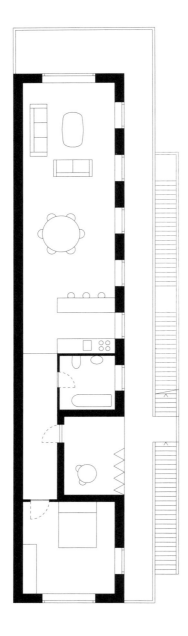
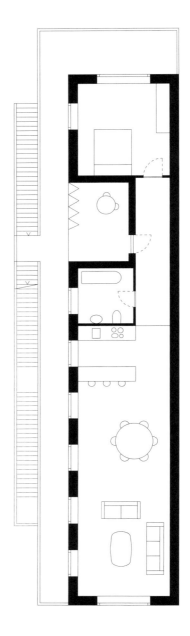

36

Private City Laboratory EAST

Scale 1:200

Charline Dayer

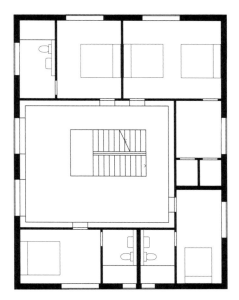

Laboratory EAST   Private City

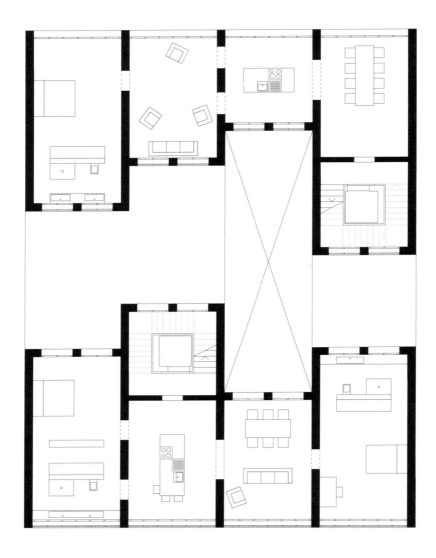

Scale 1:200

Benjamin Gmür

Laboratory EAST Private City

43

Aline Grossrieder

Scale 1:200

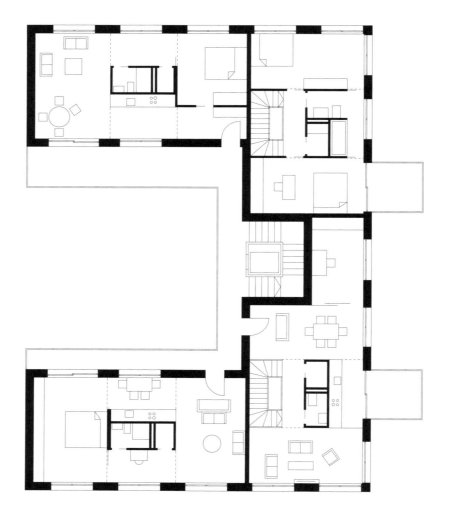

44

Private City Laboratory EAST

Scale 1:250

Julius Henkel

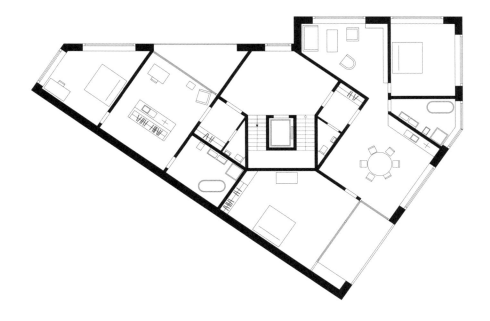

Laboratory EAST   Private City

47

Helena Esteves Lopes

Scale 1:200

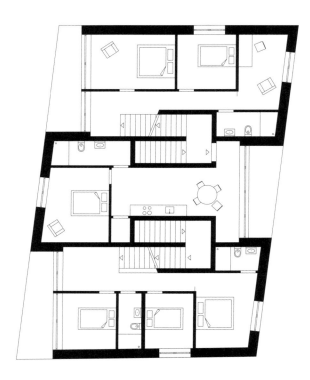

Private City   Laboratory EAST

Scale 1:200

Elena Lurati

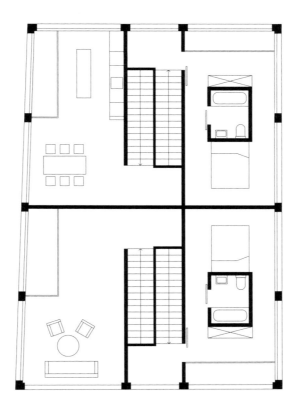

Laboratory EAST   Private City

Amira Mahfouz

Scale 1:200

52   Private City   Laboratory EAST

Scale 1:200　　　　　　　　　　　　　　　　　　　　　　Adrien Meuwly

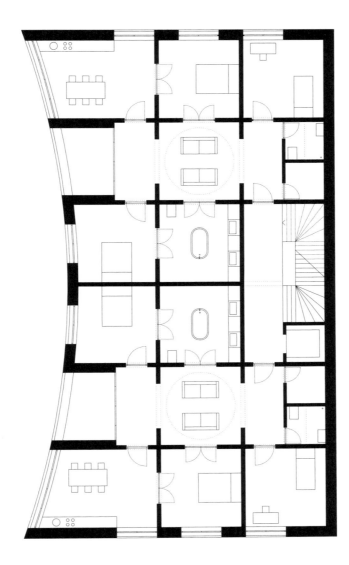

Laboratory EAST　　Private City　　　　　　　　　　　　55

Adrien Muller

Scale 1:200

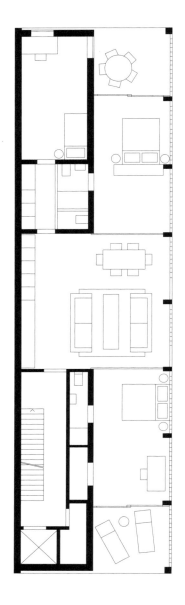
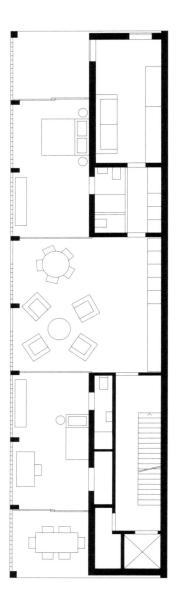

56 — Private City — Laboratory EAST

Scale 1:200

Pierre Nebel

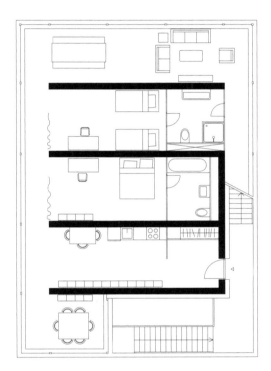

Laboratory EAST Private City

59

Julia Nahmani

Scale 1:200

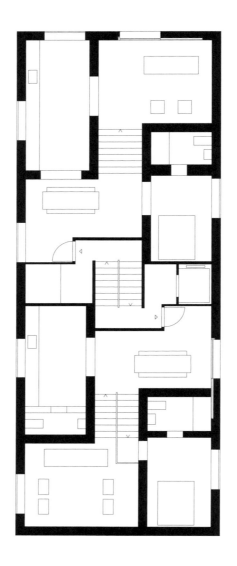

60

Private City Laboratory EAST

Scale 1:200

Felix Parpoil

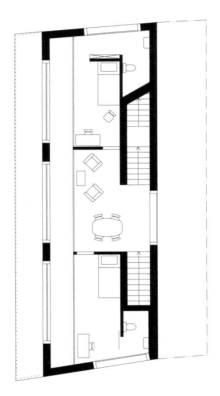

Laboratory EAST Private City

63

Alessandra Patarot

Scale 1:200

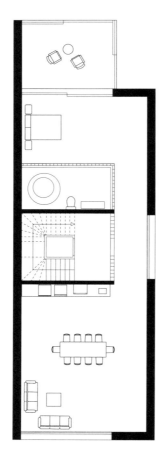
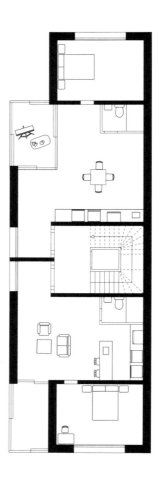

64

Private City

Laboratory EAST

Scale 1:200

Christophe Pittet

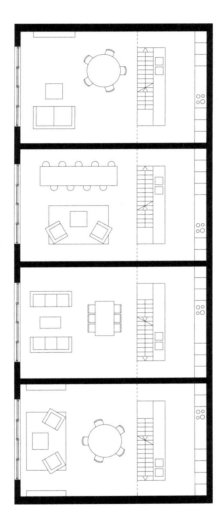

Laboratory EAST   Private City

67

Charlotte Prins

Scale 1:200

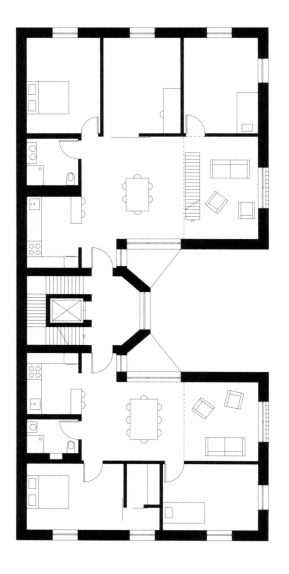

68

Private City

Laboratory EAST

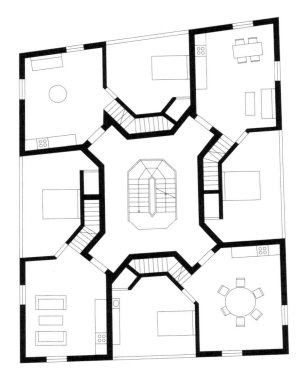

Sébastien Sartorio

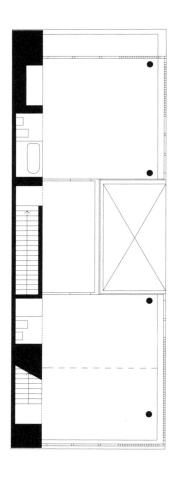
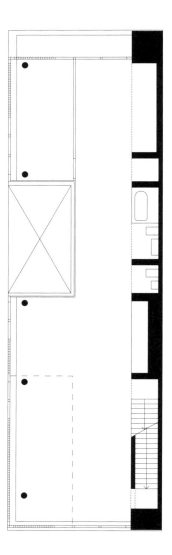

Scale 1:200

Bertran Suris

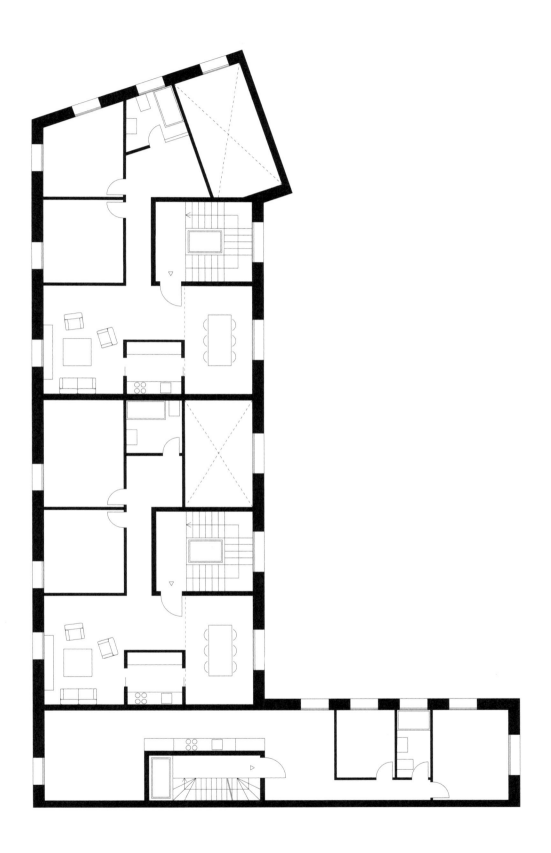

Laboratory EAST   Private City

75

Bastardo Studer

Scale 1:200

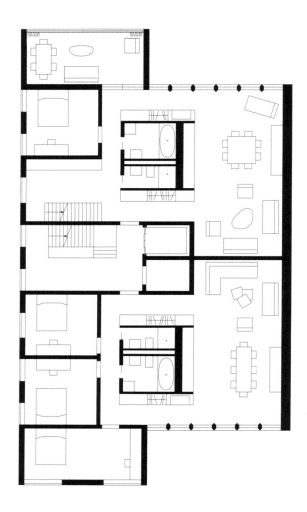

76   Private City   Laboratory EAST

Scale 1:200

Xenia Vennemann

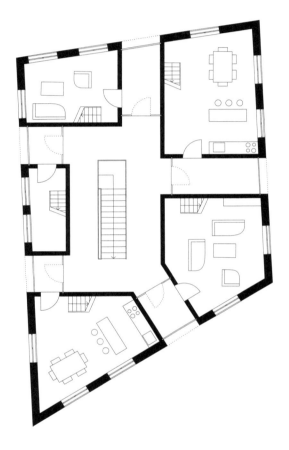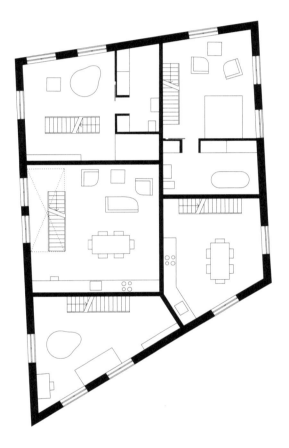

Laboratory EAST Private City

Charles Vieillecroze

Scale 1:200

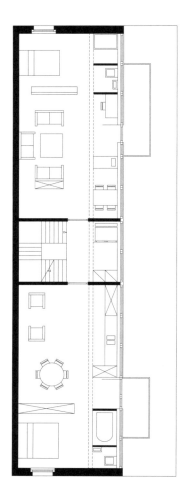
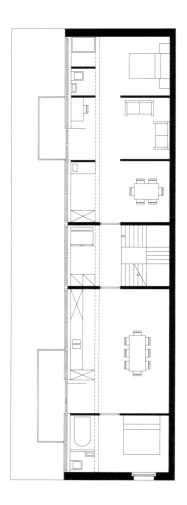

80

Private City Laboratory EAST

Scale 1:200　　　　　　　　　　　　　　　　　　　　　　　　Julia Widmann

Laboratory EAST　　　Private City

Delimiting Dwelling: The House, the Apartment and the City

Approaches to Liberating Urban Living

Klaus-Dieter Weiß*

Despite all that has been written on the subject, the history and development of housing is only superficially about "apartments". Very rarely are people enthralled about a "house" because of the apartments it contains. On the other hand, no apartment, no matter how perfect, can compensate for the shortcomings of the "house".

The "house" in question is in fact two "houses" that, for the residents, differ in one very important respect. One of them contains one, at the most two dwellings; the other, several or many apartments. One of them epitomises the popular incarnation of a happy, contented private life; the other is barely even noticed in its capacity as a "house".

The components of which the two houses are composed are, to all intents and purposes, identical: living areas, ancillary spaces, green space, utility rooms, play areas and so on. However, in one case, the individual components are formed into a complex, interwoven system of spaces that together constitute more than the sum of the individual parts. In the other case, the elements remain separate specific entities within an arbitrary organisational structure.

> "A house must be like a small city if it is to be a real home; a city like a large house if it is to be a real city." Aldo van Eyck, 1959[1]

The lack of adequate networking at an urban scale that Christopher Alexander lamented back in the 1960s, at the same time as Alexander Mitscherlich's criticism of "the inhospitability of our cities",[2] resulted in significant disparities in the distribution of housing across the city.

Aside from a person's social and sociocultural background, it is the dualism between the "house" (the single-family home) and the "apartment" (a high-rise dwelling) that determines his or her opportunity (or lack thereof) to freely assert their place in their surroundings and to stake a claim to it. The examples shown outline the primary criticism of multi-storey housing as the repetitive addition of cell-like private dwellings, a criticism that persists to the present day. Three lines of development underline this pattern, irrespective of time, place or type of building. The path from the private space of the apartment to the public realm of the street and the city leads in each of these examples through a no-man's-land of formally and functionally minimised circulation elements, like stairs, landings and corridors. It seems that most people's popular notion of a home is not compatible with multi-storey living. At any rate, there is no demand and the market therefore responds with no supply.

The dream of the single-family home that we encounter almost wherever we turn epitomises a standpoint that is so prevalent that it is worth investigating its origins.

> "[...] the private home, shielded from the incalculability of the outside world, has become an ideal for all of society that few are able to achieve to such a degree, and many more will never see. The problem is that it has become the benchmark for modern living and for housing policy. In the private home, people can live their lives with their family on their own terms."
> Hans Paul Bahrdt, 1979[3]

A house, therefore, creates autonomy, whereas an apartment sets constraints. A house symbolises independence and individualism but an apartment, by comparison, is merely a stopgap. The marketplace has long settled the competition between these two extremes of the spectrum of housing options. The public has not only voted "pro villa" but also against the magnificent monuments "for consumption",[4] in other words "contra architecturam".

The need for a more comprehensive examination of the apartment is not new: one need only think back to CIAM in 1933 and to the criticism voiced in the 1960s.

> "Today's architectural 'products' only offer technological or aesthetic variations on familiar forms of appropriating space without ever calling such forms into question. Put simply: if we want to develop a comprehensive program for investing our intellectual, scientific and technological potential in the sensible design of our living environment, we must not only free ourselves from certain preconceived models but also venture beyond the urban schemes they give rise to. And we need to devise and establish entirely new forms of taking possession of space."
> Jacques Bardet, 1969[5]

The response of the architecture group SITE (Sculpture In The Environment) was to stack single-family homes in a high-rise framework. While more symbolic than practical, it neatly portrayed the mental dilemma within the profession. Many years before, in 1924, Josef Frank had also reached this same conclusion. Unlike Le Corbusier, however, he resigned himself to the fact and saw no way of integrating new forms of housing within the existing fabric of the city.

> "We have been striving to find ways of making living in these kind of houses [i.e. multi-storey buildings] more similar to that of living in a house with a garden, and in the process to find a new form for these houses. But all the proposals made so far, which now need trying out – terraced houses and small apartment buildings born out of the ideas of recent years – have not been built due to a lack of money." Josef Frank, 1924[6]

> "The 'Highrise of Homes' Project is based on the premise that apartment dwellers need the unique advantages of garden space and personalized architectural identity offered by freestanding 'houses' within the dense environment of a multi-story structure." SITE, 1982[7]

The genealogy of SITE's innovation can be traced back to the year 1909, in which *Life Magazine* published a cartoon that indulged the fantasy of the house dweller still more, presenting an altogether more spacious, more individual idea of aerial living. Rem Koolhaas, who reproduced the cartoon in his book *Delirious New York*[8] and thus probably provided the inspiration for SITE's reinterpretation, notes that the architectural journals of the time were still devoted to the high-flying plans of the Beaux-Arts.

SITE's drawing now hangs in the Museum of Modern Art. The emphasis here is on the drawing as a commentary; a country mansion on the eighteenth storey is not a realistic proposition in Manhattan.[9] All the same, it begs the question as to whether the apartment block need resort to such blatant imagery in order to compete with and present alternatives to the single-family home, itself a form of dwelling not above criticism. Could it be that Le Corbusier really was the last great revolutionary in this still-relevant question of modern civilisation? Or can we simply offload the responsibility for the design of our cities and dwellings onto the shoulders of the people and turn our attention to building ground-level single-family houses, as Heinrich Tessenow, Roland Rainer, Christoph Hackelsberger and others have done?

> "If we are not able to redistribute land to create the basis for a biologically superior housing form, and to replace apartment buildings with single-family houses, we will let a unique opportunity to improve the health of our urban environments slip through our fingers." Roland Rainer, 1944[10]

Apartments today continue to pander to the dream of the house. They offer a higher standard of living than ever before, both in terms of floor area and technical fittings. But, compared with other achievements made this last century, the promise of "à la carte living" – the mass product of apartment dwelling – seems positively antiquated.

High-rise of homes – how one lives and the house one lives in

The provision of housing is based on two basic but quite dissimilar and mutually exclusive principles: house building on the one hand, and housing – apartment building – on the other. The dissolution of the unity of house and dwelling gave rise to two quality categories.

> "With the present importance of the city [of Rome] and the unlimited numbers of its population, it is necessary to increase the number of dwelling-places indefinitely. Consequently, as the ground floors could not admit of so great a number living in the city, the nature of the case has made it necessary to find relief by making the buildings high." Vitruvius, c.33 BC[11]

The "superior" dwelling therefore occupies a house in its entirety, while the "inferior" dwelling lies next to, beneath and above other dwellings, and is merely part of a house.

This image of contrasts – on the one hand the happy autonomy of the (single-family) house and on the other the constraints of the (multi-storey) apartment – is so firmly anchored in the collective mind's eye that any attempt to disband this dualism seems futile. Consequently, this simple differentiation between house and apartment dominates demand as it does supply. It would seem that every living situation can be described as either house or apartment, as individual or collective; no further explanation required.

> "The pseudo country house sits uneasily in its shrunken countryside, neither quite cheek by jowl with its neighbour nor decently remote, its flanks unprotected from prying eyes and penetrating sounds. It is a ridiculous anachronism. The view from the picture window is of the other man's picture window. The bare unused islands of grass serve only the myth of independence. This unordered space is neither town nor country." Serge Chermayeff and Christopher Alexander, 1963[12]

Factors such as the size and layout of an apartment, or the qualities of the site or the immediate urban environment, are, it seems, almost inconsequential when compared with the straightforward fact that one lives in a house of one's own in supposedly independent surroundings.

Even the spiralling building costs, which limit private homeowners in their freedom of choice, causing ever more to choose off-the-shelf designs, only serve to focus attention on this key difference in the competition between the models of the house (= single-family house) and apartment (= multi-family house). It is the house that matters most of all, not the apartments within it. How one lives is a factor of "the house one lives in", not the "apartment one lives in". If this is true, then it would appear that residents are, consciously or subconsciously, more interested in the space between the dwellings than the dwellings themselves. Conventional multi-storey apartment buildings offer too little choice, and the standard constellation – entrance to staircase, stairs, landing, door left, door right, more stairs, and so on – does nothing to dispel this impression.

> "It is human nature to look at things; we have to learn to see the spaces between them." Wolfgang Metzger, 1936[13]

If living space is created by separating off a private zone from a publicly accessible area, the quality of the dwelling is not determined just by the standard of the space set aside for living in (the apartment) but to a large extent by the boundary that separates as well as relates the private zone of the apartment to the other parts of the building.

In the dream of an own home, on the other hand, it is always a complex interplay of indoors to outdoors, building to plot, degree of enclosure and exposure.

From the most intimate corner, the sleeping area, to the boundary between one's own territory and that of one's neighbour or the street, homeowners are generally able to determine the degree to which they wish to mesh private and public. Regardless of how enclosed or exposed he or she chooses to live, they are largely free to determine how they, and their own private territory, should interact with their spatial and social environment. The freedom offered by this kind of house or building is in practice rather more limited, as most typical estates of single-family homes create little in the way of a public realm. Consequently, there is little in the way of community. Nevertheless, this degree of self-determination is still seen as the best of all available possibilities.

In the case of the apartment, the money spent on housing generally covers not just the private space of the apartment but also a proportion of the house and its outdoor spaces, including all given boundaries and transitions. Nevertheless, the influence one has as an individual ends at the door of the apartment. Residents are rarely given the opportunity to extend their private sphere into their immediate spatial and social surroundings as they please. Given the fact that when subdividing a house into several neighbouring dwellings the design and use of non-dwelling spaces can lead to conflict between the parties within a house, this space, and with it any scope the residents may have to shape their surroundings, is intentionally minimised. Although supposedly for cost reasons, the upshot is that the influence one has is usually restricted to the apartment.

> "An apartment is likely to be more profitable – for all parties, both landlord and tenant – if it caters for its residents' basic needs. These include not just the living requirements per se but also straightforward opportunities to strike up relationships within the surroundings, in the building, at work, on the street, as well as, if one so wishes, to withdraw and remain anonymous. We also know, though, that in the current climate, and due to a lack of awareness both in society and in politics, such lofty ideals are condemned to remain unfulfilled." Alexander Mitscherlich, 1968 [14]

The residents of scattered settlements, or even of more compact housing estates on the outskirts of cities, quickly become more privacy-oriented than they had perhaps planned to be when they originally decided to live there. In the absence of adequate opportunities to interact with others in the public realm, and therefore having only the possibility of indirect contact with others – and here the shortcomings of the house (single-family home) are on a par with those of the apartment (multi-family building) – the homeowner turns his or her attention inwards to the private realm. As a result, the special quality of ground-floor living, namely the ability to open one's private realm onto the world outside, is often underused.

> "Modern communication systems bring, fragmented and fleetingly, glimpses of phenomena and sounds never before seen or heard. Man is in touch with the whole world without moving from his seat. But the man next door with different tastes, often expressed in diverse and loud noises is all at once transformed from desirable neighbour into intrusive stranger. The suburb pays no attention to these closely linked overwhelming changes, and pretends to be a village of closely-knit neighbours and friends. The men, women, and children of suburbia are seldom quite together, and never quite alone."
> Serge Chermayeff and Christopher Alexander, 1963 [15]

In this respect, the sterile anonymity of a high-rise building, despite the unavoidably cramped nature of its access ways, which most people nevertheless rather tolerantly accept as being "normal", can also be described as exhibiting a degree of quality of life.

> "The loss of the private sphere and of ensured access to the public sphere is characteristic of today's urban mode of dwelling and living, whether technological and economic developments have quietly adapted the old forms of urban dwelling to new functions or new suburban settlement forms have been developed on the basis of these experiences." Jürgen Habermas, 1962 [16]

The trend toward the single-family home, a factor of the relatively high quality-of-living situation (autonomy, environmental quality, contact with nature) and the high social prestige it promises, is also a product of the disadvantages of multi-storey living, which weigh far more heavily than house-dwelling.

In reality, both forms of dwelling lack variety in the transitional areas at the boundaries of the dwelling. It is just that the single-family home has a better means of escape through the ability it provides to withdraw into the privacy of the home.

Communities against the rest of the world

The focus of housing programmes on the "inner" qualities of apartments at the expense of their "external" qualities is ultimately evident in the end results. It is also reflected in the pattern of consumer demand and in the widespread habit of documenting housing schemes by focusing on floor plans to the exclusion of almost everything else. This remarkable blind spot in the professional study of housing is, however, a reflection of the more general and widely documented residential value scales. The role of the individual dwelling within the wider context of the organisation of the house and its surroundings is of lesser importance.

An Austrian study from the year 1973 did at least differentiate clearly between areas "within the apartment" and those "outside of the apartment", establishing a value ratio of 70:30.[17] Aside from that, however, the building was still seen as little more than a container for the individual apartments. Of the desirability criteria given for areas outside the apartment, 13% of the overall score was accorded to location factors (emissions, infrastructure), 15% each for the "relationship to outdoor areas at ground level" and "play areas for children", with just 2% for community facilities, which included everything from common rooms to car parking. By comparison, "ease of furnishing" was accorded more weight than all of the external factors put together. Even trivial details such as the kitchen and bathroom fittings, which change over time and are often adapted by the resident, ranked higher than the relationship of an apartment to its outdoor surroundings.

"[...] I imagine these apartments [in apartment buildings] as having two storeys with an entrance from the street. My proposal, overall, would be something that looks like a terraced house, with a stair outdoors from which one can reach the different terraces. These terraces could be called elevated streets. Each person possesses his own entrance with his own outdoor space where he can sit at the end of the day and take in some fresh air. It is possible for children to play on the terrace without worrying about being hit by a car." Adolf Loos, 1931[18]

Unlike, for example, the experiments of the utopian socialists, the conditions and prerequisites for community-oriented housing do not usually pervade the entire building in its organisation and appearance. Instead, they content themselves with adding isolated communal rooms and spaces to an otherwise distinctly conventional building structure. This fails to address both the desire to create community and the possibility to withdraw into one's private space. Then again, neither of these aims can be realised at the scale of a high-rise building. Private, community-oriented and public realms can only be realised by overcoming the no-man's-land of the lifts, staircases and corridors. This is a problem that can also be seen in a similar form in Le Corbusier's Unités d'Habitation. The image of the ocean liner with its minimised and predominantly dark access corridors is likewise not a recipe for repression-free and community-oriented living in a house of such dimensions.

"The tenement creates discipline through isolation. A tenement is a tenement regardless of whether in a rearward courtyard, part of long terraced building, a high-rise or an elegant luxury-service high-rise. The tenement is first and foremost the property of its owner, then the living environment of its residents and must therefore present a coherent frontage. And it must be 'beautiful' in a joyless way, i.e. orderly and clean. To this end, house rules stipulate that washing may not be hung out to dry above the height of the balustrade because it could disturb the 'orderly' appearance." Walfried Pohl, 1974[19]

"The widespread 'dream of real life' goes back to our historical way of living: the village as the centre of life, where people do things together, have communal spaces and places to meet – and one's own dwelling which also provides some degree of green space for personalisation. Where do we find this in modern-day mass housing? The key main elements are an apartment with some green space, and communal areas where one can play together, partake of sports and converse with one another." Ernst Gehmacher, 1983[20]

It is striking just how simple these proposed solutions seem to be. The specific quality of the single-family home is reduced to the fact that it has a garden. This, in turn, can be just as easily replaced by a balcony. The spectrum of human interaction is reduced to an idyllic image of village life. And this community will instantly form as soon as one provides some communal spaces within the building. If things were that simple, we need only equip Bijlmermeer in Amsterdam and the Märkisches Viertel in Berlin with balconies of five square metres (= single-family house typology), and green areas, covered communal spaces and swimming pools on the roofs (= village character) to be able to fully satisfy the needs of their residents. What one can say is that two of these criteria, for example the green areas and the covered communal areas (see, for example, Walter Gropius, Franz Roeckle and Wilhelm Riphahn's buildings for the Dammerstock housing project in Karlsruhe), do at least guarantee a better standard of living.

The general assumption here is that residents will inherently want to be in touch with their neighbours and community, and that they will want to expand their personal circle of friends to include them. The dream of the single-family home is proof that this is by no means automatically the case.

Community-oriented housing can therefore only be one option among many. As such, these housing models and experiments do have their place. Whether this can be successfully realised with the combination of high-rise plus communal facilities must be seen in each individual case.

Privacy, sociability ... civilisation

"The rug finds it easier to be colourful than the picture, the picture easier than the house, the house easier than the life within it."[21] The rug, picture and house have never been more "colourful" than they are today. Architecture must strive, as Ernst Bloch says, to concentrate on life.

As impressive as the images of Gottfried Böhm's Züblin building in Stuttgart may seem, its vast hall remains empty. It symbolises and embodies the size of the company it houses but has no relation to life, even less to the city.[22]

A comparison with Böhm's housing project on Berlin's Fasanenplatz[23] underlines this discrepancy, despite their differences due to the constraints of the existing block structure. Here too the entrance hall is opulently designed, but almost all of the apartments turn away from it. Aside from the kitchen, WC and storage room, only two of three living areas afford a glimpse of it. The absolutely regular floor plan of the gallery, on the other hand, recalls Walter Gropius's far simpler but in principle similar gallery-access housing in the Dammerstock estate in Karlsruhe. There too, it was already apparent that the width the gallery offered residents little space for personalisation. The same approach can be seen in Jean-Baptiste André Godin's design for the Familistère in Guise. There are few pointers that the aspect of communal life plays a role in everyday life. Böhm's original idea gave far more weight to the communal interior of the building, with large spaces within an extended hallway area and informal transitional areas between the private areas and the communal hall (he also included a fourth apartment to minimise the distance to the neighbouring building). Why not give the residents more opportunity to influence the communal areas when the site is so obviously suitable?

> "In general we may say that the regulating participation in human interaction forms a part of the building task. Buildings and cities both divide and bring together human beings, and 'milieus' fitted for different public (or private) activities are created." Christian Norberg-Schulz, 1963 [24]

Most common multi-storey housing typologies juggle a number of aspects, including the number of storeys and form of the house, but also the aspect of "access", although here it is usually technical aspects that are the focus. Little attention is accorded to the ability of residents to personalise and appropriate this communal space. In the same way that apartment plans are rated according to quantitative criteria such as floor area, storage space, quality of fittings, etcetera, architects strive to make circulation and access corridors a clearly legible part of the building's organisation. As such, a gallery is a gallery is a gallery, whether in James Stirling's Runcorn housing, in Aldo Rossi's Gallaratese or Ralph Erskine's Byker Wall. Each of these carefully measured typologies gives the impression of providing a wide range of different living forms.

The semblance of public space between the "isolated" private dwelling and the "isolated" consumerism-oriented urban realm of the pedestrian zone does not become truly public through its design as a grand staircase, or through the provision of equally "isolated" communal facilities on or in front of the building. For Richard Sennett, this is the mark of what he calls an "uncivilised society".

> "[Camillo] Sitte's generation conceived of community within the city; today's urbanist conceives of community against the city."[25]

The users of an apartment that already provides for an introverted style of living (in the positive sense of the word) are therefore not interested in a small capsule attached halfway up an otherwise featureless staircase. All this provides is another form of privacy that relates to itself, not to the private realm of the apartment and not to the public realm of the city. Such confused interpretations, as seen in many so-called alternative models and proposals for "housing frameworks", among them projects by SITE, Yona Friedman[26] or Frei Otto, cannot be a model.

> "Modern society is ready for extreme projects, kilometre-high housing landscapes for millions, monumental works such as that of Paolo Soleri, so long as one condition is fulfilled: an inviolable, undisturbed private realm." Frei Otto, 1973 [27]

Would it not generally make more sense for architecture to address the relationships between the residents of a building than to explore flawed compromises? Could not the typology of housing developments take a qualitative step forward and make the residents the centre of attention, creating new housing variants within the spectrum of privacy-oriented, community-oriented and publicly-oriented housing? Can we provide residents with choices as to how they wish to define the boundary to the private realm? Providing opportunities for residents to contribute to the spaces outside the immediate limits of their apartment increases the quality of life to a greater degree than is possible through the addition of ever more cost-intensive "extras" inside the apartment. While it is true to that the funding available for housing is increasingly limited and that rents are rising steadily, one may ask whether it makes sense in the long term to use public funds to finance stopgap solutions when it would also be possible, with a slight additional outlay and a shift in priorities, to provide a better quality of living that residents would in turn be willing to invest in themselves – in the same way that they would do for a single-family home – despite the disadvantages that come with it.

The dilemma in the additive combination of several dwelling units – in contrast to a house with just one dwelling – that one cannot flexibly respond to the residents' different relationships to their surroundings can be addressed by focusing attention on the "territorial environment" of the dwelling, either at the level of the storey or of the building as a whole. The resident can therefore make choices according to their own preferences. The argument that this exceeds the residents customary experience of living can be levelled at any new alternative that exceeds convention, whether inside the apartment (flexible floor plans, split-level or maisonette apartments, and so on) or outside (gallery access, tenant's gardens, and so forth). The decision to purchase a single-family home is likewise an adventure involving risks of its own: once made, the decision to live in a particular form of housing is hard to reverse given the financial investment made.

Individual examples of schemes that are breaking away from the functional monotony of additive urban housing are beginning to demonstrate the feasibility of these deliberations in practice. For example, the privacy-oriented approaches of Jeremy and Fenella Dixon, most apparent in their starter flats in London's Lanark Road,[28] or of James Stirling in his luxury town housing in Manhattan.[29] The community-oriented approach can be seen very clearly in the renovation of the Galéries Barbès in Paris by the architects Jacques Lévy and Christian Maisonhaute,[30] and to a lesser degree – in part due to the complexities of the situation – in Ralph Erskine's Byker Wall. The public-oriented approach, in which a private apartment has a direct transitional zone to a public street, can be seen in the work of Aldo van Eyck's urban redevelopment in Zwolle or Herman Hertzberger's residential street project in Amsterdam.[31] As each of these projects is very much a product of their specific conditions, they can only serve as examples rather than as models.

At this point it is worth recalling how Charles Fourier's pupil Victor Considérant once defined the aims of housing:

> "It is not about buildings huts for the proletariat, houses for the burghers, and villas for speculators or the nobility: it is about building a palace in which people can live." Victor Considérant, 1847[32]

A modern-day version of this vision for a democratically grounded "palace" would, in the words of Adolf Arndt, require "an individualised differentiation of spaces",[33] not just in terms of their form but also their function.

> "The task of democratic architecture is to enable every person to be who they are and to have a place in society. [...] Should there not be a relationship between the public principle of democracy and the inner and outer transparency and accessibility in her public buildings?"
> Adolf Arndt, 1960[34]

Should not the houses of the city likewise be part of the public and social life of the city? After the hygienic reform of the city must come a second liberation, namely of housing from its socio-spatial constraints.

* This is an abridged and edited version of Klaus-Dieter Weiß's essay "Grenzenloses Wohnen: zwischen Wohnung, Haus and Stadt", first published in Günter Fischer, et al., *Abschied von der Postmoderne: Beiträge zur Überwindung der Orientierungskrise*, vol. 64 in the series *Bauwelt Fundamente*, eds. Ulrich Conrads and Peter Neitzke (Braunschweig/Wiesbaden: Friedr. Vieweg & Sohn, 1987), pp. 101–60. This current English version has been translated by Julian Reisenberger. The format of the footnote apparatus has been amended to match the current publication, but in terms of abbreviated entries has not been correspondingly supplemented. The images accompanying the original essay have likewise been largely cropped to match, but the captions are those in the original.

1 Aldo van Eyck, cited in Josef Lehmbrock and Wend Fischer, *Von Profitopolis zur Stadt der Menschen* (Munich, 1979), p. VI/9.

2 Christopher Alexander, "Die Stadt ist kein Baum", *Bauen + Wohnen*, 7 (1967); Alexander Mitscherlich, *Die Unwirtlichkeit unserer Städte* (Frankfurt a.M., 1965).

3 Hans Paul Bahrdt, "Über das private Wohnen in unserer Zeit", in Lehmbrock and Fischer, *Profitopolis*, p. 196.

4 cf. Monique Seyler, "Städteplanung und Gesellschaftsklassen", in *Architektur Extra* (Frankfurt a.M., 1971), p. 112.

5 Jacques Bardet, "Die Revolution im Städtebau hat noch nicht stattgefunden", in *Architektur Extra* (Frankfurt a.M, 1971), p. 238.

6 Josef Frank, "Volkswohnhaus und Individualismus", *Der Neubau*, 11 (1924), p. 118.

7 SITE, *Highrise of Homes* (New York, 1982), p. 47.

8 Rem Koolhaas, *Delirious New York* (New York, 1978), p. 69.

9 cf. Klaus-Dieter Weiß, "Landsitz auf Manhattan, 18. Etage", *Bauwelt*, 29 (1982), p. 1,174.

10 Roland Rainer, *Die zweckmäßigste Hausform für Erweiterung, Neugründung und Wiederaufbau von Städten* (Breslau, 1944), pp. 23–4.

11 Vitruv, *Zehn Bücher über Architektur* (Darmstadt, 1976), p. 115.

12 Serge Chermayeff and Christopher Alexander, *Gemeinschaft und Privatbereich im neuen Bauen* [first published 1963] (Mainz, 1971), pp. 57–8.

13 Wolfgang Metzger, *Gesetze des Sehens* [published 1936], (Frankfurt a.M., 1975), p. 31.

14 Alexander Mitscherlich, "Was soll aus unseren Städten werden?", *Bauen + Wohnen*, 3 (1968), pp. 81–2.

15 Chermayeff and Alexander, *Gemeinschaft und Privatbereich*, p. 58.

16 Jürgen Habermas, *Strukturwandel der Öffentlichkeit* [first published 1962], (Neuwied/Berlin, 1976), p. 190.

17 Urs Hettich, "Qualitätsmodelle und ihr praktischer Einsatz", *Wohnbauforschung*, 5–6 (1973), p. 35.

18 Adolf Loos, "Die moderne Siedlung", in *Trotzdem* [first published in 1931], (Vienna, 1982), pp. 205–6.

19 Walfried Pohl, "Die reduzierte Architektur: das Dilemma des modernen Städtebaus", *Der Architekt*, 11–12 (1974), p. 281.

20 Ernst Gehmacher, in *Wohnbau*, 9 (1983), p. 14.

21 Ernst Bloch, *Spuren: 1910–29*, cited in *Stadt*, 11 (1982), p. 30.

22 cf. *moebel interior design*, 10 (1985), p. 48.

23 cf. Arbeitsgemeinschaft "Bauen in der Innenstadt", *Bauen in der Innenstadt* (Berlin, 1983), n.p.

24 Christian Norberg-Schulz, *Logik der Baukunst* [first published 1963] (Braunschweig, 1980), p. 120.

25 Richard Sennett, *Verfall und Ende des öffentlichen Lebens: Die Tyrannei der Intimität* [first published 1977] (Frankfurt a.M., 1983), p. 331.

26 Yona Friedman, "Konzept einer Grünen Architektur", in Ekhart Hahn (ed.), *Siedlungsökologie* (Karlsruhe, 1982), p. 80.

27 Frei Otto, "Die Europastadt" [first published in 1973], in Frei Otto, *Schriften und Reden: 1951–1983* (Braunschweig/Wiesbaden, 1984), p. 111.

28 cf. *archithese*, 5 (1983), p. 27; *Architectural Design*, 5–6 (1983), p. 18.

29 cf. *International Architect*, 5 (1981), p. 27; *Architectural Design*, 7–8 (1980), pp. 11–12/31.

30 cf. *Baumeister*, 5 (1981), p. 474; *L'Architecture d'Aujourd'hui*, 209 (1980).

31 cf. *L'Archltecture d'Aujourd'hui*, 225 (1983), p. 56.

32 Victor Considérant, *Destinée sociale*, (Paris, 1847), p. 419, cited in Franziska Bollerey, *Architekturkonzeptionen der utopischen Sozialisten* (Munich, 1977), p. 124.

33 Adolf Arndt, *Demokratie als Bauherr* (Berlin, 1961), p. 21.

34 Ibid., p. 20.

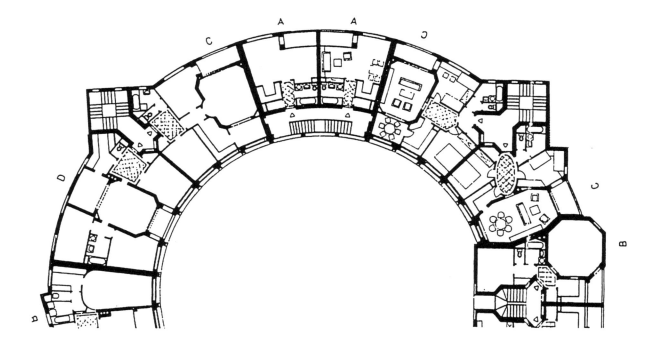

Rob Krier, Wien, 1985

From historicism ... to postmodernism for example: Henry Roberts, London, 1848; Eugène Viollet-le-Duc, Paris, 1861; Otto Wagner, Vienna, 1881; Frank Lloyd Wright, Chicago, 1895; Auguste Perret, Paris, 1902; Antoni Gaudí, Barcelona, 1905; Peter Behrens, Berlin, 1920; Michel de Klerk, Amsterdam, 1920; Henri Sauvage, Paris, 1922; Kay Fisker, Copenhagen, 1923; Johannes Duiker, Den Haag, 1926; Karl Elm, Vienna, 1927; Ludwig Mies van der Rohe, Stuttgart, 1927; Walter Gropius, Karlsruhe, 1928; Otto Haesler, Kassel, 1929; Arne Jakobsen, Copenhagen, 1930; Guiseppe Terragni, Milan, 1934; Van den Broek and Bakema, Hengelo, 1950; Candilis-Josic-Woods, Bobigny, 1957; Oswald Mathias Ungers, Cologne, 1959; Alvar Aalto, Porvoo, 1966; Faller, Schröder and Frey, Marl, 1967; Ralph Erskine, Helsinki, 1981; Ricardo Bofill, Paris, 1981; OMA, Amsterdam, 1983; Gustav Peichl, Vienna, 1984; Rob Krier, Vienna, 1985; Fisker, Kopenhagen, 1923; Johannes Duiker, Den Haag, 1926; Karl Elm, Wien 1927.

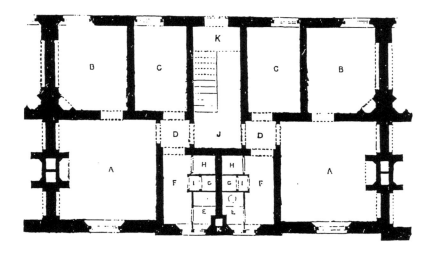

Henry Roberts, London 1848.

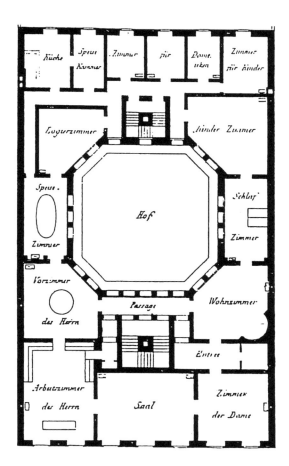

Karl Friedrich Schinkel, 1826.

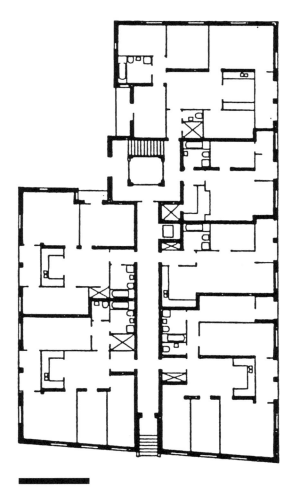

Aldo Rossi, Berlin, 1984.

Despite innovations in apartment design, the design of the circulation areas (stairs, landings and corridors) remains as mediocre as ever.

From 1826 to 1982 ... for example in Berlin: Karl Friedrich Schinkel, 1826; Carl Wilhelm Hoffmann, 1847; Alfred Messel, 1894; Hermann Muthesius, 1909; Bruno Taut, 1925; Erich Mendelsohn, 1926; Heinrich Tessenow, 1928; Hugo Häring, 1929; Fred Forbat, 1930; Walter Gropius, 1955; W. Luckhardt and H. Hoffmann, 1955; Hans Scharoun, 1956; Egon Eiermann, 1960; Frei Otto, 1964; Josef Paul Kleihues, 1971; Jürgen Sawade, 1978; Hinrich and Inken Baller, 1980; Richard Meier, 1980; Rob Krier, 1980; Oswald Mathias Ungers, 1981; Raimund Abraham, 1982; Bruno Reichlin and Fabio Reinhart, 1982; Aldo Rossi, 1984.

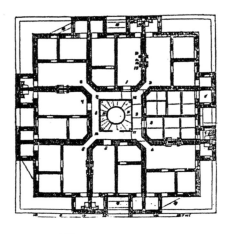

Worker's housing, London, 1818.

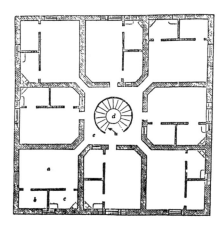

Public housing for workers in England, 1843.

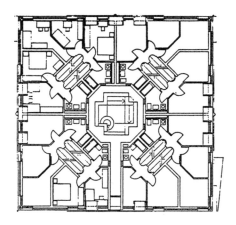

Schneider-Wessling, apartment building, Berlin, 1984.

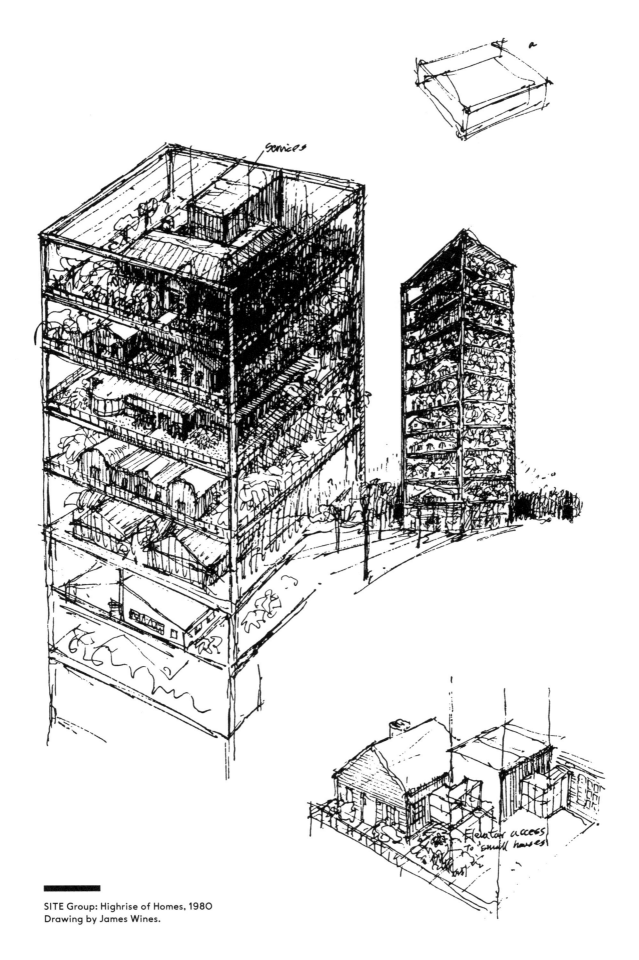

SITE Group: Highrise of Homes, 1980
Drawing by James Wines.

A building with houses, 1920.

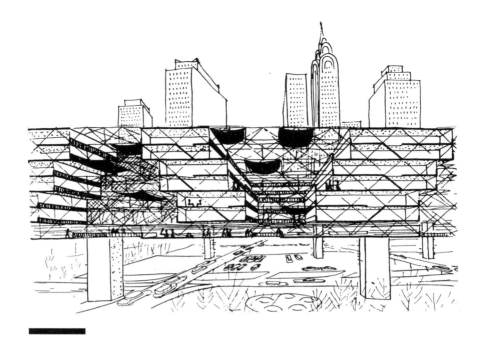

Yona Friedman, storeyed spaces elevated over the city, overlooking the city, 1956.

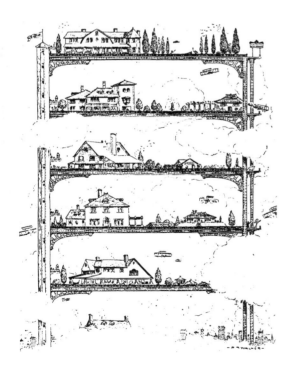

Housing framework with 84 storeys (Life), 1909.

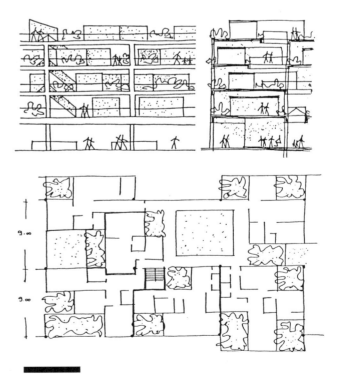

Yona Friedman, private storeyed spaces with apartments and a garden on each floor on each storey.

Laboratory EAST   Private City

Chapter 2

The Best Home

Influenced by Stanley Tigerman and his project *The Best Home of All* for the 1979 MoMA exhibition *Buildings for Best Products*, the design studio explored the potential for densifying existing showrooms and cathedrals of consumption. Simultaneously, the students focused on the cooperative model as a legal framework deeply rooted in Swiss society to develop their housing extensions and to foster the idea of the "house as a city" and the growing importance of hybrid building types.

Laboratory EAST　　The Best Home

Stanley Tigerman's *Best Home of All* was the starting point of the design studio Best Home, where students were asked to address the universe of consumerism and its built embodiment in Switzerland.

The Best Home for All

Tiago P. Borges

In 1979, the Museum of Modern Art invited six architects – Robert M. Stern, Anthony Lumsden, Michael Graves, Charles Moore, Allan Greenberg and Stanley Tigerman – to participate in the collective exhibition *Buildings for Best Products*. In the opening text of the catalogue, Philip Johnson briefly reviewed the six projects for a showroom for the "Best", and rehearsed a broader historicist conclusion: "The Modern Movement seems really gone from the scene. But not modern architecture. Modern can still include Venturi; Hardy, Holzman, Pfeiffer; Wines – as well as our six. Harder to define than the International Style, less arrogant and self-satisfied with their moral superiority than their ancestors, architects today are more inclusive, more permissive, more popular-oriented, indeed more popular, than the Modern Movement allowed."[1]

Under the title *The Best Home of All*, Stanley Tigerman presented an ironically serious project that Johnson described as "the glorification of the split-level Colonial ranch house."[2] Tigerman's proposed building was similar in every way to the typical American suburban house, except for its unusual size. Every element was a skewed magnification of its standard scale: the front step was 32 inches (81 centimetres) high, and the front door was 12 feet (3.65 metres) wide and more than 26 feet, 8 inches (8 metres) high. Everything was Gulliver-sized, a quality that in the estimation of the MoMA's curator made it a project capable of competing with the Big Duck on Long Island so celebrated by Robert Venturi. In his proposal, Tigerman addressed the issue of identity, firmly anchoring it in the "American dream".[3] For the Chicago architect, the suburban house was as Americanly iconic as television, the only disturbance being the "alien element" of the shopping mall.[4] The answer to creating a real "comfortable place" – the "Best Home of All" – was to reconcile these poles: the average American should be able to shop in an environment as familiar as his or her own home. By facetiously marrying these two glorified American symbols – the suburban house and the shopping mall – Tigerman not only lays bare the issues of living and consumption but in so doing critiques the complex subjects of identity in American society and the idea of American territory. His simultaneous focus on scale in architecture is almost a kind of *détournement* Pop, all of what he proposes being lathered in bubbles of sarcasm: "they had finally found an American symbol right there where they least expected it – at home in the suburban United States of America – and all the snotty bastards in the urban United States were simply green with envy."[5]

Tigerman's *Best Home of All* was the starting point of the studio Best Home, where students were asked to address the universe of consumerism and its built embodiment in Switzerland. The studio explored the programatic potential of existing structures through the lens of the Migros supermarket chain, considering both its context and also the company's overall adminwistrative framework. This cooperative model – one that has long been officially anchored and promoted in Switzerland – formed the basis for new housing scenarios, designed to simultaneously reformulate the traditional shopping experience. The proposed exercise required the students to examine existing superstores, not only in terms of how they function but also in terms of current social, economic and territorial realities. A number of these superstores were analysed using criteria such as their geographical position, their infrastructure, the existing functions of adjacent buildings, and also the knock-on status of adjacent housing. The aim was to establish what the existing typologies or characteristic local urban patterns were and to take them into account during the process. Although the core of the programme was to design new housing solutions, the students were also meant to address the issue of densification, in the sense that it constitutes a sustainable spatial countermeasure – urban or rural – to militate against the lack of development sites and high land prices.

The intention was that the proposed structures plug into an existing superstore, thereby establishing a new programmatic environment with the ability to combine multiple elements into a single complex structure. However, the students were given no specific project programme: the ultimate goal was to establish a 24-hour use cycle by imagining designs with the capacity to reconfigure the existing infrastructures with ever-changing programmes – a quasi mixed-use and space-sharing conceptual framework. This scheme allowed students to either challenge existing norms or to mine any potential programmatic symmetries. Whilst in order to reduce the distance between the producer and user some of the resulting proposals also integrated production as part of the consumption cycle, others critically addressed contemporary neighbourhood political issues and existing programmes by proposing a housing solution for migrants on the rooftop of an existing superstore. The concept behind this was that the migrants work for and are paid by the shopping-centre company as a form of integration within their new community.

By framing only the narratives, the project parameters deliberately refrained from pre-establishing set strategies for the extensions and add-ons, meaning that the solutions formulated were correspondingly varied. If there is a common denominator in all the different projects that emerged, it has to be an optimistic boldness to strive not for the "Best Home of All" but rather the "Best Home for All".

1/2 Philip Johnson, "Forward", in The Museum of Modern Art, *Building for Best Products* (New York: The Museum of Modern Art, 1979), p. 7.

3 Stanley Tigerman, "The Best Home of All", in Ibid. pp. 22–4.

4/5 Ibid. p. 22 / Ibid. p. 24.

Scale 1:500

Candice Baldy & Romain Thiébaud

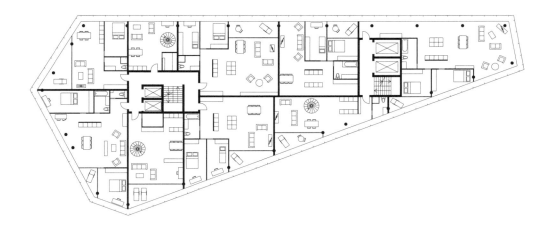

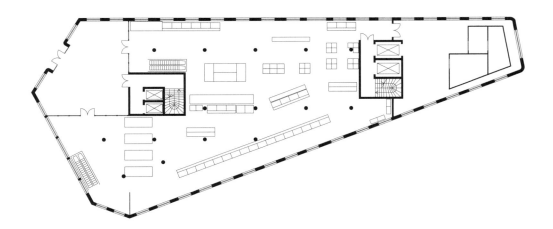

Laboratory EAST   The Best Home

103

Antoine Béguin & Valentin Rey

Scale 1:500

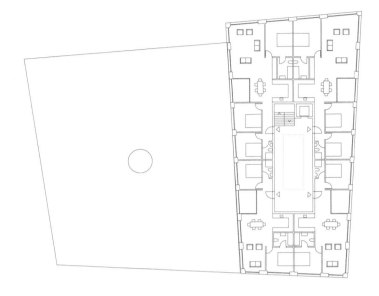

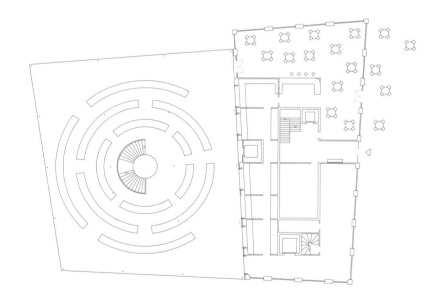

104   The Best Home   Laboratory EAST

Scale 1:650

Marlon Biétry & Marc Vertesi

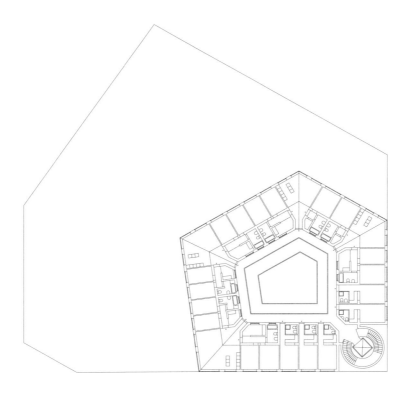

Laboratory EAST The Best Home

107

Victoria Bodevin & Margaux Ruiz

Scale 1:500

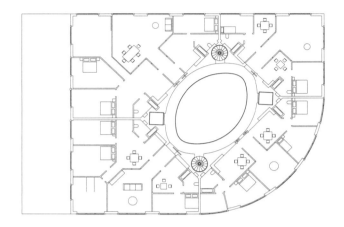

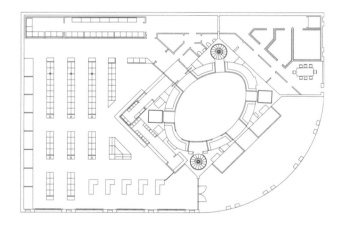

The Best Home · Laboratory EAST

Scale 1:650

Félix Caspary & Léa Gauchoux

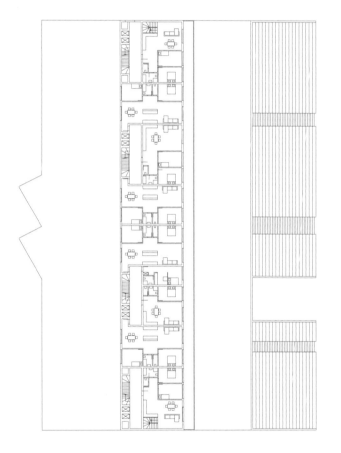
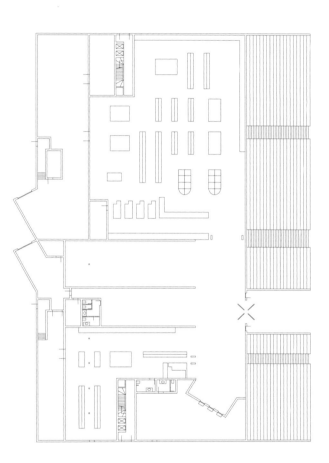

Laboratory EAST　　The Best Home

111

Gabriel Chareton & Théophile Legrain

Scale 1:500

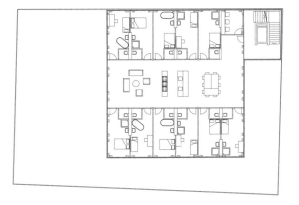

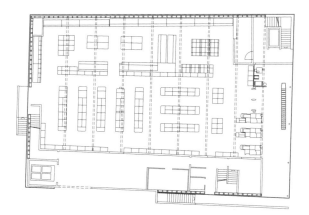

112   The Best Home   Laboratory EAST

Scale 1:1000 — Léonard Darbellay & Sami Farra

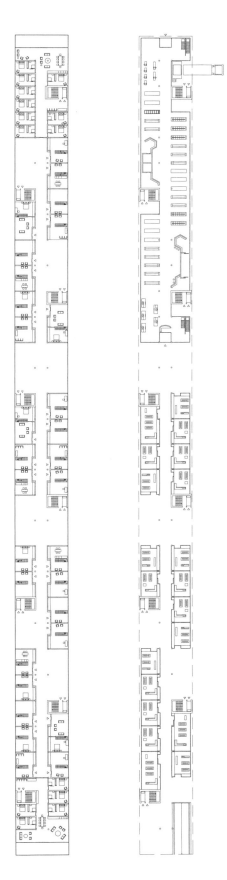

Laboratory EAST — The Best Home

115

Sophie Di Rosa & Marc Reymond

Scale 1:1000

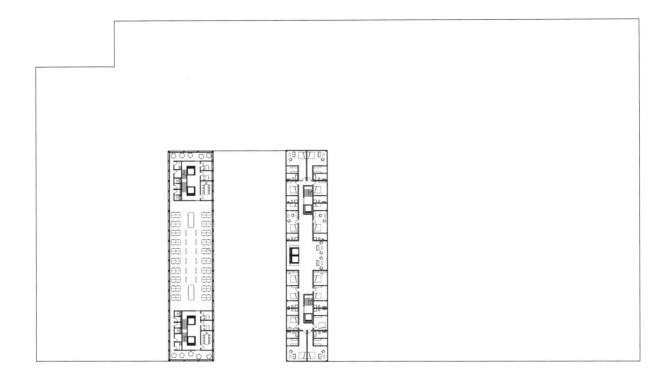

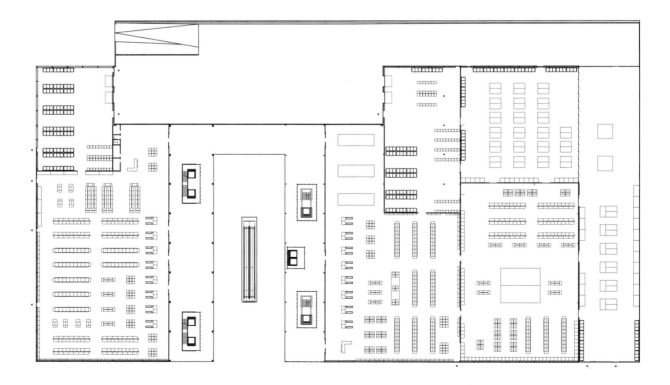

The Best Home — Laboratory EAST

Scale 1:650 — Gabriel Disner & Tim Pham

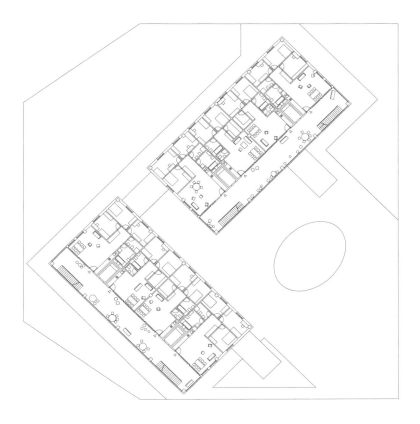
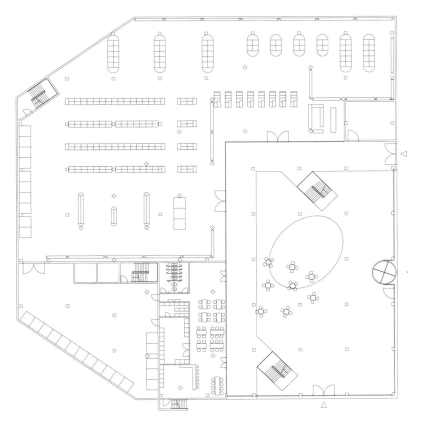

Laboratory EAST — The Best Home

Christopher El Hayek & Teo Vexina Wilkinson

Scale 1:500

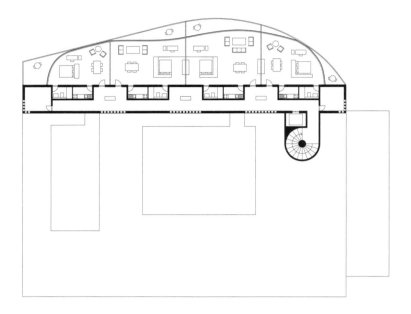

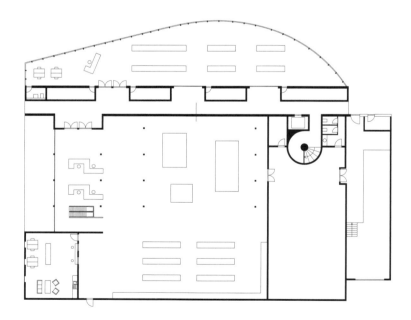

120   The Best Home   Laboratory EAST

Scale 1:1000   Marc Evéquoz & David Richner

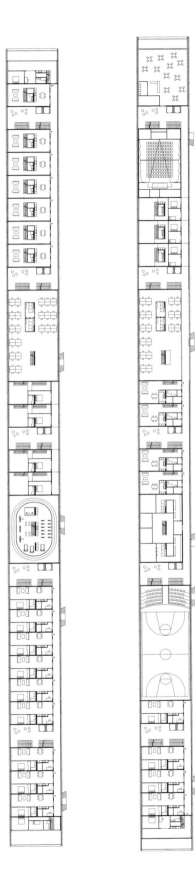

Laboratory EAST   The Best Home   123

Juliette Jancu & Afroditi Maloukotsi

Scale 1:750

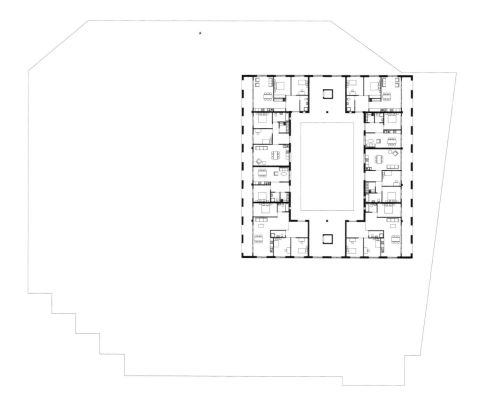

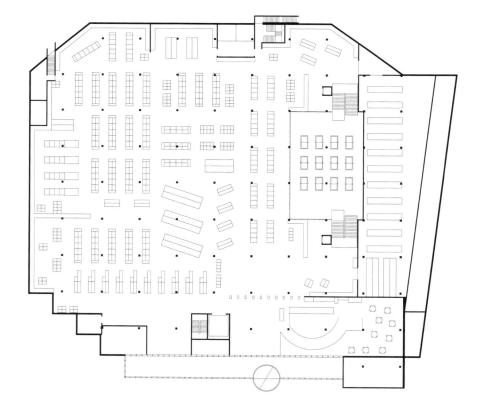

124

The Best Home

Laboratory EAST

Scale 1:650 Charles Jenny & Gentian Kadrijaj

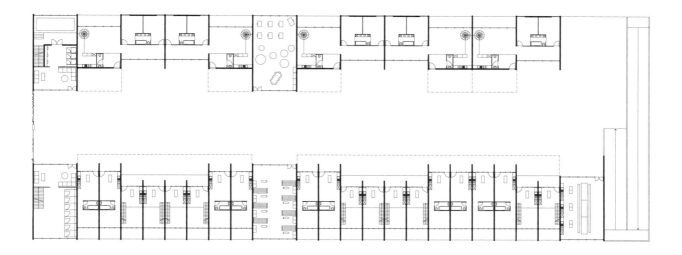

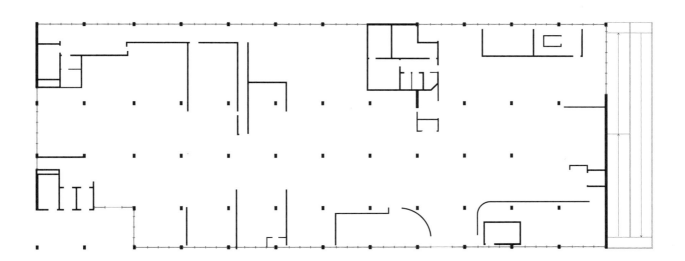

Chloe Joly-Pottuz & Justine Rausis

Scale 1:500

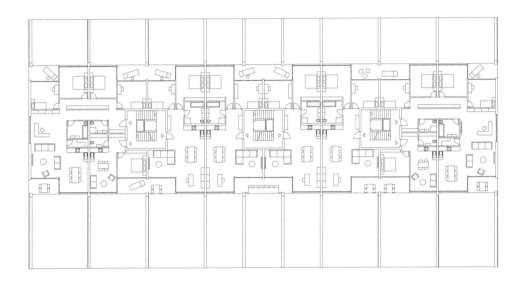

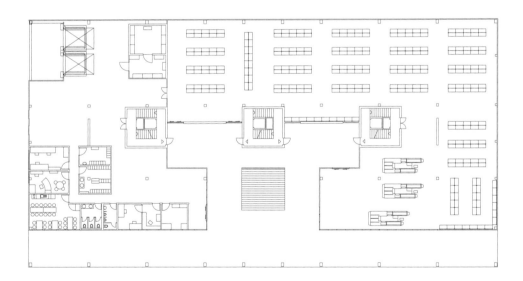

128   The Best Home   Laboratory EAST

Scale 1:1000   Alexander Karpushov & Killian Worreth

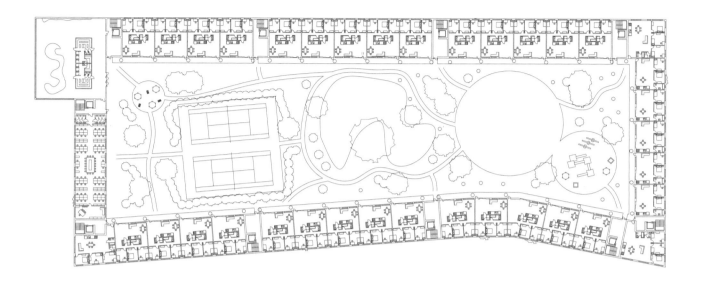

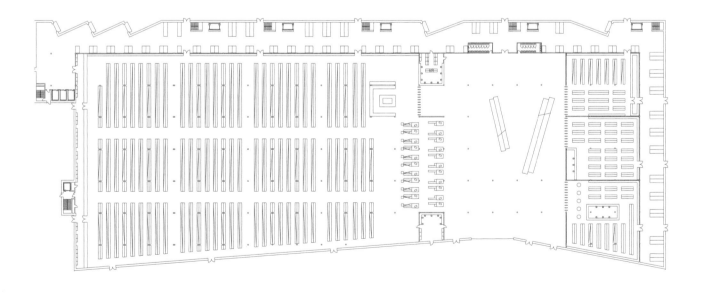

Laboratory EAST   The Best Home

Alexandra Liebich

Scale 1:1250

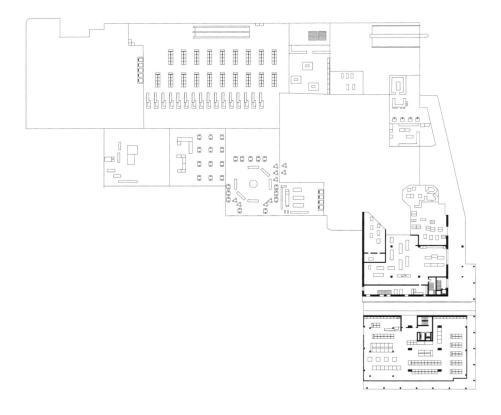

The Best Home — Laboratory EAST

Scale 1:500

Diane Stierli & Marine Wyssbrod

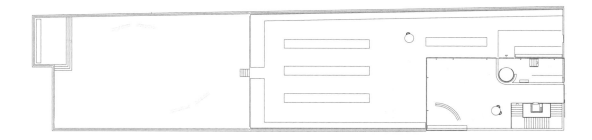

Laboratory EAST The Best Home

135

Laura Stoll & Ursina Ziörjen

Scale 1:1750

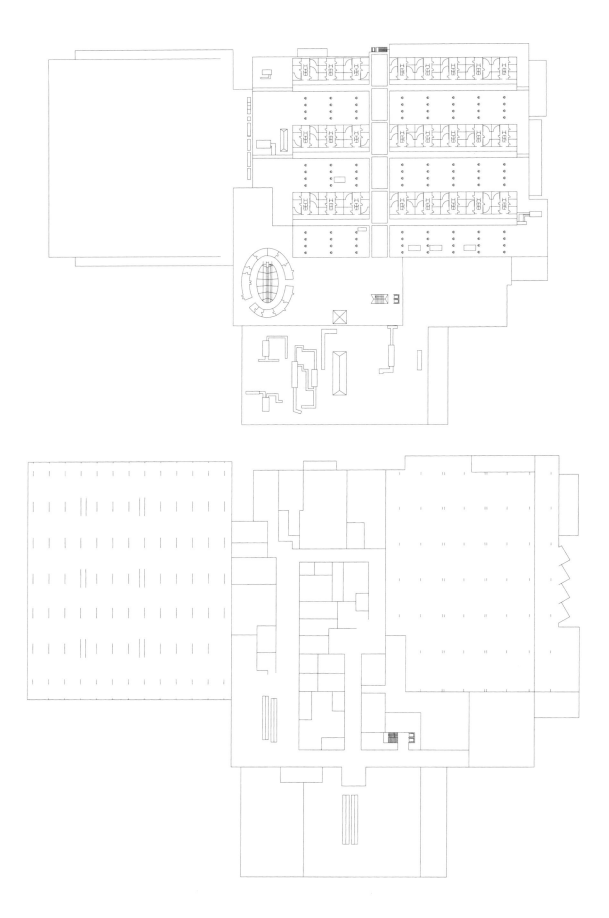

136   The Best Home   Laboratory EAST

Supermarket Superhome

Antje Bittorf

In 1985, in an essay entitled "Hybrid Buildings" issued in the series *Pamphlet Architecture*, Joseph Fenton published a homage to a building type that at the time had already almost completely disappeared from the American townscape and had become all but forgotten.[1] His attempt to outline a definition of hybrid buildings, and to classify and catalogue various examples built in metropolitan cities in the USA at the end of the nineteenth century, can be understood as a manifesto for functionally mixed and functionally diverse cities. In contrast, the later makeup of post-Second World War cities came to be shaped by the urban principles of the CIAM congresses, whereby functional zoning and suburbanisation were the new ideals. Those who could afford to moved out of the city centres into a house in the green suburbs – a model that was replicated endlessly. The car, once a symbol of luxury, became a mass product, affordable for most families. While the man of the house went to work in the city, his wife used the car for shopping and errands in the suburbs. The American Dream was born. At the same time, inner cities were increasingly zoned into specific functional areas: into business districts on the one hand, and mass housing estates for the underprivileged on the other, which before long became social black spots with high crime rates.

Largely neglected by urban planning policy, the inner cities of the U.S. in the 1980s – at the time Fenton's article was published – had lost much of the appeal that they had once embodied at the outset of the 20th century as a symbol of progress and technical innovation. The development of elevators, central heating and air conditioning from the 1880s onwards, as well as of new construction techniques, had made it possible to build taller and taller buildings in response to rapidly rising land prices. The massive floor areas of high-rise buildings could accommodate seemingly endless combinations of different functions. Apartments, offices, museums, theatres, shopping centres, banks, railway stations – all the key elements of modern nineteenth-century cities – could be incorporated into this specifically American building type, a model that flourished until the global economic crisis from 1929 onwards. For Fenton, the hybrid urban block symbolised a model for the revitalisation of the American inner cities of the 1980s, and his catalogue was intended as a source of inspiration for architects and urban planners.

What Fenton misjudged, however, was the extent to which the built reality had changed in the meantime. Urban sprawl had transformed the face of the American landscape to such an extent that it was no longer reversible. Vast networks of motorways and freeways extended across country, and the once vertical metropolitan cities had long since been eclipsed, both in significance as well as in sheer surface area, by expansive horizontal urban conurbations. But here too, it was still possible to find hybrid building types incorporating multiple functions: shopping malls, for example – a building type conceived entirely to meet the needs of a mobile consumerist society. The elevator that once extended public space vertically into the skyscrapers of Manhattan had been eclipsed for decades by the car, its fundamental role unmistakably evident in the huge parking lots that surrounded shopping malls. Nevertheless, just as their vertical predecessors had done, these vast flat buildings, located at strategic nodes in the networks of motorways connecting these new horizontal conurbations, contained a host of different urban functions – shops, restaurants, petrol stations, childcare facilities, post offices, banks, cinemas – and the mall itself had become a meeting place, a setting for urban life. Only one function, however, remained separate: housing.

Instead, shopping malls positioned themselves as distinct surrogate centres in a sea of single-family homes – a situation that Stanley Tigerman parodied in his contribution to the *Buildings for Best Products* exhibition at the MoMA in 1979. For him, the single-family home in the suburbs epitomised typical American values, presenting an idyllic picture interrupted only periodically by the overt capitalism of the shopping halls. His *Buildings for Best Product* showroom contribution was, consequently, a larger-than-life copy of one of the surrounding single-family houses. A huge housewife, modelled after Mary Tyler Moore, greeted shoppers at the door, who entered the interior via a half-open garage door. The customer effectively never need leave home. The "Best Home" becomes the "Best Showroom": shopping mall and house meld into a single organism. "Of course, the very BEST thing about this new home is its neighbourliness: It's an American Symbol right there where it's least expected – at home in the suburban United States of America."[2]

As simple and provocative as Tigerman's response was, the question remains as to why these two functions have never melded into one in (American) reality, despite not only being direct neighbours but also despite the fact that, from a cultural and historical perspective, housing has always been a deeply hybrid configuration? Housing has traditionally united several functions under one roof: dwelling, cooking, the keeping of livestock, trade, craftsmanship, storage, to name but a few. Indeed, until well into the eighteenth century, even individual rooms in house were hybrid spaces, usable in different ways and serving diverse functions. Rooms had no predefined function: if one wanted to eat, food was served on a table that was brought in and then removed again afterwards. Even sleeping was not tied to a specific room. The dwellings of the lower classes were similarly flexible, though for a different reason: the lack of space and the prevalence of poverty meant that a single room often had to serve all the necessary functions of a dwelling.

Why, then, should we not attempt to combine the shopping mall with housing? The ecological and economic advantages are obvious: the strategic location of supermarkets at traffic intersections offer excellent accessibility, while the extensive level floor area of supermarkets is easy to extend vertically, increasing density and reducing further land consumption, and the direct proximity of housing and commerce reduces journey times and fuel costs. If one were to intelligently combine the spatial qualities of both functions, a new building type could arise out of the horizontal metropolitan conurbation – one that responds to the needs and realities of the twenty-first century and offers a new housing alternative for today's mobile society. The strategy of revitalising neglected city centres by reintroducing functionally diverse spatial concepts into focal locations is without doubt advisable and sensible. Many young people now move to the city precisely because of these urban qualities. A greater problem by far, however, is how to deal with both new and existing commercial sites on the periphery and the mono-functional housing estates in the suburbs that are increasingly incapable of responding to the changing demographic situation. In terms of their sheer area, these two building types are a much greater problem. This is where the Best Home approach can offer new impulses to the age-old question of where and how we want to live in the future.

---

1 Joseph Fenton, *Hybrid Buildings*, published as *Pamphlet Architecture N°11*, ed. Lynnette Widder (New York and San Francisco: Princeton Architectural Press, 1985), pp. 1–46.

2 Sarah Moolman Underhill (editor), *Stanley Tigerman: Buildings and Projects 1966–1989* (New York: Rizzoli, 1989), p. 97

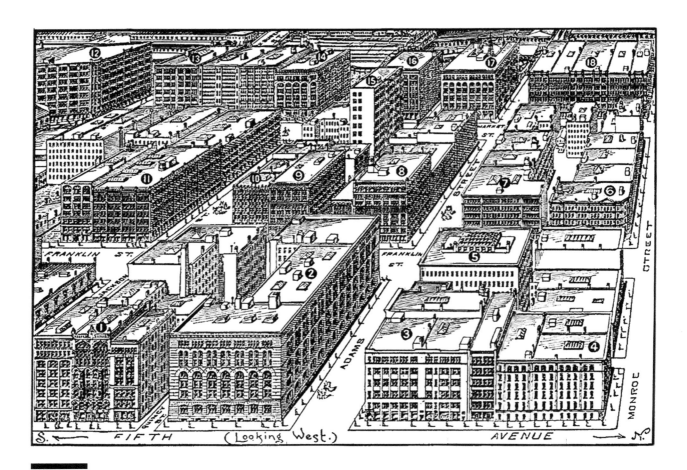

View of Chicago, 1893

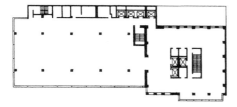

James Stewart Polshek and Partners, 500 Park Tower, New York, 1983. Typical apartment floor and typical office floor

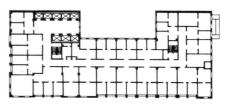
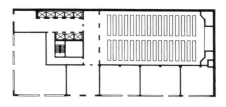

Holabird and Roche, Chicago Temple, Chicago, 1924. Typical office floor and ground floor

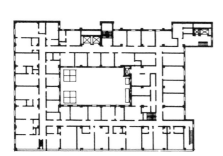
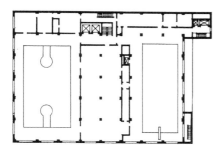

Wm. B. Ittner & Brueggeman Assoc., Missouri Athletic Club, St Louis, 1916. Typical bedroom floor and fifth floor

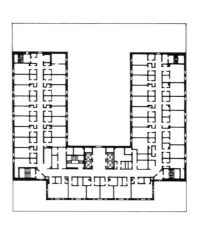
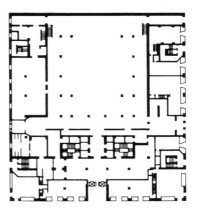

Zantziger, Borie and Medary, Pen Athletic Club, Philadelphia, 1928. Typical bedroom floor and fifth floor

Laboratory EAST The Best Home

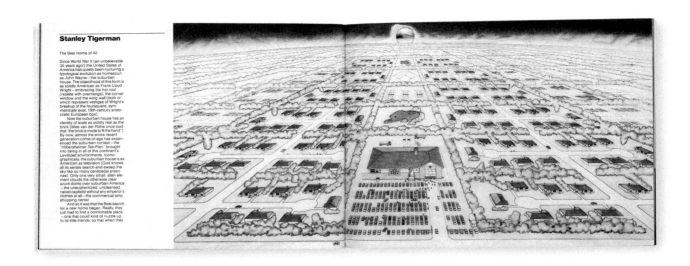

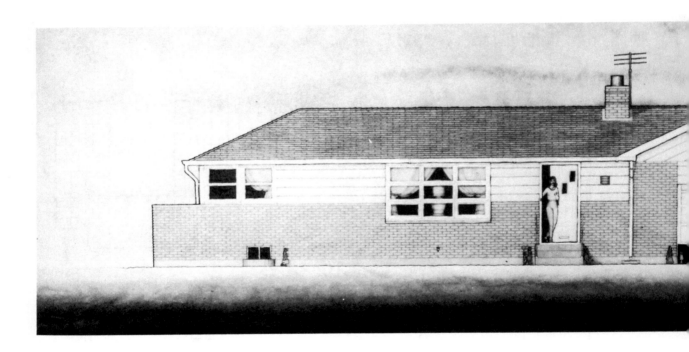

Stanley Tigerman, *The Best Home of All*, 1979: (above top) overall situation layout; (above) elevation of the main building; (right, top to bottom) the building shown with seasonal decorations – Halloween, Christmas, Easter and the Fourth of July

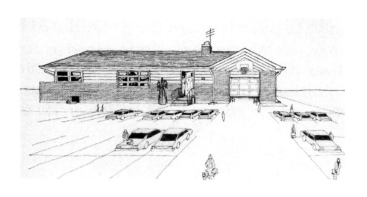

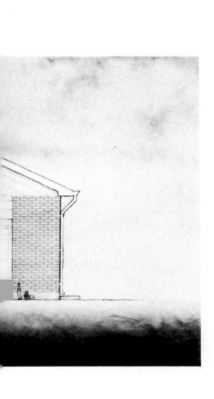

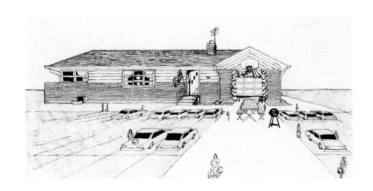

Laboratory EAST   The Best Home

The dismantling and demolition of the headquarters of the International Olympic Committee in Lausanne presented a pragmatic opportunity to push forward the potential of reuse in architecture within an academic context. Made likewise out of reused materials, the goal was to design and build an art pavilion that would serve as an exhibition space for Le Cabanon – an association for contemporary art – on the campus of the University of Lausanne.

Cabanon Art Pavilion

Photographs
Sebastian F. Lippok

2016

Chapter 3

The Best Room

The purpose of the design studio was to study the importance of the ground plan as a spatial composition of different living uses. Transcending technical functions, the focus of the studio concentrated on the room itself — the base unit of the plan. The research was divided into two stages. A set of noteworthy references was compiled and used to make a selection of rooms, which were then separated from their respective floor plans to be analysed and rebuilt as models. Here, the focus was placed on the elements that limit the space and the elements that significantly shape the characteristics of the room. The rooms were moulded in plaster and the void became matter — a sculpture-like form. During the second study step, students analysed the representation of interior space in art paintings. The aim was to generate new narratives in the expectation that new fictional architectural projects would result from unexpected interplays of rooms.

2014

In the design studio Best Room, our specific interest lies in the room itself as the smallest unit of architecture: as an elementary aspect of designing architecture and as a core focus of architectural teaching and practice.

Good, Better, the Best

Anja & Martin Fröhlich

"For the best is, here or there, surely waiting to be found",[1] writes Johann Wolfgang von Goethe, characterising Faust's restless search for the best as an inner motivation that drives mankind as a whole. As a superlative, "the best" is essentially a constructed ideal: as soon as we achieve our objective, based on our new level of experience we feel obliged to improve on it anew. To this extent, it would be more accurate to say that mankind strives to achieve something better, whereby "better" means in relation to that which has been achieved to date. The ideal of "the best" is, therefore, a more or less utopian point of reference that we can never reach, but that nevertheless serves as the starting point for every attempt to better a situation. In effect, "the best" is a frozen optimal state of something, rooted in a particular circumstance or temporal sequence and that is subject to renewal over time as conditions change. In design processes, we can identify two strategies for determining the best solution: the method of optimisation and/or the method of selection. Using the optimisation method, we continually alter an existing, found situation, deploying the means and possibilities available to us until it embodies the best possible solution for our requirements. In the selective method, we choose from a range of pre-existing, similar variants of one and the same thing. Through a process of comparison, we discover the best conceivable solution. Both strategies aim to achieve the best possible result—the best possible compromise between different parameters or different qualities under the given conditions.

What, then, represents "the best" in the realm of architecture? What defines its optimal state? For centuries, beauty, harmony and the sublime were championed as the qualities that denote what is best in architecture. Historically, architects strived for correct dimensions, harmonious proportions and universally ideal forms. Today too, exemplary architecture also aims to embody qualities such as perfect form, permanence and presence. Then as now, compelling architecture has been characterised by a specific approach to materials and construction. Likewise, a precise response to location, to function and the masterly organisation of social relationships are factors that set apart excellent architecture from superficial or arbitrary buildings. These criteria serve not only as a measure of what constitutes good architecture but act as a basis for its very conception.

In the Best Room project, our specific interest lies in the room as the smallest unit of architecture: as an elementary aspect of designing architecture and as a core focus of architectural teaching and practice. The Best Room project is, therefore, an opportunity to examine the conceptual development of a room or the idea of a room and its articulation.

The Best Room – a project

Architecture creates, shapes and structures space. Space is the elementary medium of architecture. To create optimal spatial structures, functions and relationships, we must first analyse space and the conditions that inform it. What we regard as the "best room" in architecture depends on the kind of problem posed and the solution we expect could solve it. In the project itself, we explored what constitutes the best living room in the context of a dwelling, as represented by its architectural expression and its atmospheric quality. To help identify a system of values, we undertook two different analyses: one of floor-plan typologies, to better understand functional relationships; and a second of so-called negative-space models, to explore the cubature and presence of rooms.

(a) Understanding and analysing space:
To begin with, the design studio examined the cubature of model rooms through an analysis of historical examples, whereby the respective room for analysis was first located within the context of a given floor-plan composition using the selective method. This room was then extracted from the existing floor plans, analysed and made in the form of a model of the interior. The focus here lies on elements that define the room and inform its key characteristics, such as the proportions of the room, the thickness of the walls, connections between walls, thresholds, reveals, the articulation and placement of doors and windows, and any elements situated within the room.

(b) Researching and completing space:
In a second step, the design studio examined refer-

ence examples of rooms in historical paintings depicted as domestic scenes of living. These fragmentary representations served as the starting point for exploring the idea of the room, which the students then used to complete the remainder of it beyond that framed in the picture. Even the most rudimentary depictions proved to contain the information needed to complete the space: its structure, proportions, details and illumination. Our specific architectural interest here was in the portion of the room not shown in the portrayal, namely the idea of the completed room as a whole and the fictitious dwelling within which it is situated.

(c) Designing and constructing space:
In the final stage, the findings of the preceding analyses were used to develop the student's own idea for a room. Starting from a given situation, each student combined their own personal understanding of ways of living with the corresponding "best room" and its surrounding floor-plan composition, repeatedly reiterating it to improve on it using the optimising method. The focus here was less on the technical functions of housing than on the room as a collective and enclosed volume that is a product of its location and its possible relationships. By an internal competition within the atelier, the best "best room" from the 36 designs was selected and then built as a 1:1 timber construction on the EPFL campus.

Floor plan analysis – typologies of living-room combinations

The defining factor for the best room of a dwelling is its underlying idea – its design concept. In his book *The Production of Space*, the French philosopher Henri Lefebvre argues that "any definition of architecture itself requires a prior analysis and exposition of the concept of space".[2] With this principle in mind, the idea for a room therefore also implicitly encompasses how it relates to other rooms in a dwelling, and in turn how it facilitates social interactions: is it a predominantly communicative space or a more private space?

Its character is determined largely by its relationships to adjacent spaces and the respective ways of living it embodies. The following classifications served as a basis for the floor-plan analyses, and describe a range of different floor-plan typologies and their implications for the different connections between rooms and the corresponding implicit position of the best room within the dwelling in the student's project.

(a) The best room in a hall type:
This floor-plan typology is dominated by a central hall-like living space. As the best room in the dwelling, it is both the central space and a distributor. It is the focal space: all other rooms, including the bedrooms, open onto this space, and almost all routes within the dwelling pass through it. It is generally sizeable, as there is no need for corridors or hallways, and even private rooms are typically smaller in relation to it. As a spatial concept, it is a highly communicative space offering only limited opportunities for privacy. The idea of the best room in this hall type corresponds to that of a meeting place for the family – the "heart of the house" as seen by Leon Battista Alberti, or even Alvar Aalto's "marketplace" for living together, eating and playing with the children.

(b) The best room in an axial type:
In an enfilade, rooms are arranged in succession as a linear progression of spaces with doors at opposite ends. The best room in this floor plan typically has two doors and is transversally linked to all other spaces by a dominant axis of sight and movement. There is no separation between route and room: the way leads straight through it. The axis and doors at opposite ends means that the room extends visually beyond its direct boundaries. When the doors are open, one can see right through from the first room to the end wall or window of the last room.

(c) The best room in a corridor type:
In this floor-plan typology, rooms are arranged on one or both sides of a corridor. The corridor separates and connects the different rooms of the dwelling, including the communal living area and the individual bedrooms. As such, this floor plan creates a more or less separate and individualised way of living. The end point of the corridor is particularly significant, and ideally leads straight into the best room. This tangential form of access means the best room has just one door and therefore has a more secluded and intimate character. Originally, the corridor served as a separate, alternative means for servants to reach the main rooms, and existed alongside the enfilade. It constituted a subsidiary means of access, with layouts allowing the householders to move separately from room to room by interconnecting doors, and it was only from the nineteenth century onwards that the corridor became more popular in private dwellings and public buildings as the main means of circulation, including for the house-owners.

(d) The best room in an open-plan type – *plan libre*:
An open-plan floor plan is partitioned only by non-load-bearing internal room dividers. These free-standing walls are situated around the primary areas of movement to define spaces of different qualities. Their placement results from a study of movement patterns for the various activities in a dwelling. In this spatial concept, "rooms" are linked not by doors but by flowing space. The best room is usually in the middle, often arranged around a central element, such as a fireplace or a functional core (for instance the sanitary facilities), with other spaces arranged surrounding it. In this model, the functional relationships between the different "rooms" are the central focus, and the individual successions of spaces are accorded different characters.

(e) The best room in a single-room type – *carte blanche*:
The functionally non-specific single-room type embodies the spirit of creative freedom, and was developed in response to an ever-increasing division of functions. In this arrangement, the best room is typically perceived as a large, open space, even if structured by free-standing elements (installation cores) or adjoining niches. At the beginning of the twentieth century, this floor-plan type was comparatively widespread as a product of increasing rationalisation and a corresponding minimisation of spaces and functions. In this floor-plan type, all living functions are incorporated into a single, optimised space; often with niches that act as spatially and functionally perfected miniature spaces and that are arranged around the central single space in a manner analogous to the constellation of the hall type.

These classifications illustrate the spectrum of different concepts of living and ways of life (open/closed, introverted-/extroverted) and the respective ideas of the best room. The character of the room itself is a product of its size, proportions and form. And these aspects, in turn, relate directly to the function of the room as a space for people to reside in, for accommodating furniture and furnishings and for undertaking certain activities. Ultimately, the best room is a space for everyday use, a framework for living together, with specific characteristics that simultaneously reveal how its residents live in it.

<u>Understanding the room as a volume</u>

After the two-dimensional analysis of a room within the context of the floor plan, the design studio then considered the volumetric properties of the room. The form of an architectural space is defined by the form of the walls and surfaces that bound it, and it is these that also make a room visible by defining its perimeter. One way to make the figure of the space itself visible as a formal whole – for the purposes of analysis and to assist in understanding its spatial qualities – is to make a cast of the volume of the room, in other words of its negative space. Negative-space models are not a new method, and have been used throughout history as a means of considering interior space from outside.

The rating of space in architectural discourse is a comparatively young phenomenon that first arose towards the end of the nineteenth century, thanks largely to the work of various art historians of the period. This included people such as Heinrich Wölfflin, Alois Riegl and August Schmarsow, the latter having been the first to explicitly formulate the independent design of negative space in considering the impact of a solid body on its environment.[3] Later, the British architect Geoffrey Scott found an apt description of space as the "liberty of movement", but criticised that architects often ignored space due to its immateriality: "The habits of our minds are fixed on matter. We talk of what occupies our tools and arrests our eyes. Matter is fashioned; space comes. Space is 'nothing' – a mere negation of the solid. And thus we come to overlook it."[4]

Scott's point was that we consider space as ground and not as figure, and that we therefore only deal with it in passing. The creation of a cast of the negative space is, therefore, an exceptionally effective means of making space legible. In 1922, the architectural theorist Albert Erich Brinckmann used the means of representing negative space to clarify the effect of spaces.[5] And in 1952, the Italian architect Luigi Moretti examined the qualities of interiors deploying the method proposed by Brinckmann by using cast models.[6] This allowed him to compare the structural properties of different interior spaces and led him to assert that spatial volume has a physical presence of its own.

Our Best Room project used this same approach to identify the key criteria of room cubature, whereby the analytical exercises focused on selected living rooms, from remarkable projects, with protuberances and indentations that give them a strongly articulated volume. The craftsmanship involved in creating a cast model heightens one's awareness of the different formal characteristics of space. Simultaneously, it also consolidates and expands students' design vocabulary. The following structural qualities were revealed through the process of analysis.

(a) Geometry of a room – the spatial figure itself:
Generally, built space is defined by vertical and horizontal elements. The formal relationships between the different enclosing surfaces contain the space, making it legible as a figure. This means that any comprehension of space is dependent to a large degree on its boundaries, and therefore the room's spatial geometry. The form of a room, in turn, is mostly strongly defined by the relationship between its vertical enclosing surfaces, with the ceiling acting primarily as a mediator between the various bordering walls.

(b) Discontinuity of form:
Protrusions and indentations along the bounding surfaces interrupt the continuity of the form of a space. These are, in effect, the same as partial volumes that are added to or subtracted from the overall figure, interrupting its clear form, creating points of interest and establishing tension in the cubature of spaces, for example in the form of niches, cut-outs, bays, taller sections of space or split-level arrangements.

(c) Inserted elements that shape space:
Inserted elements that mould a room can include such items as chimney stacks, staircases, installation ducts or wall sections. Although they reduce the figure of the room by their own volume, they ideally correspond functionally and visually to it and give the room structure. When arranged so that they protrude into a space or are placed freely within it, they are legible as geometric insertions and divide a space or encourage one to circulate around them. When placed close to or adjoining the edge of a room – for example a seating niche – they change how we perceive the boundaries of the space.

(d) Surface material qualities – visible construction:
The surface qualities of a room are a product of the materials used and their respective texture and structure. Exposed material surfaces provide an indication of the underlying construction and are a valuable source of knowledge. For example, the presence of exposed beams or girders and the columns they rest on articulates them as secondary space-defining elements within a room. Our perception of a space is informed by its surface qualities, material characteristics and colours. The way a certain material is used – its specific structural characteristics – informs the design of the space, while the way a material looks – its specific expression, its visual and haptic qualities – contributes to the impression a space or interior has on us.

(e) Openings:
Openings pierce the architectonic boundaries of a space and establish a correspondence between what lies within and beyond the space. Through their placement, openings can create diverse kinds of relationships in all directions, be they visual associations or sight lines or acoustic connections. The number and size of these openings determines the permeability of a space. Visual openings in closed boundary surfaces create transparent connections between spaces or rooms that in extreme cases can make it appear as if the bounding surfaces have been dissolved.

Structurally considering the form of a space by creating a figure of its negative space makes it possible to identify the particular qualities of a room's envelope and its potential possibilities in terms of the interior. The focus therefore is always on the properties of a space as defined by the architect's design — not just its delineating surface or, the placement of elements such as walls, openings, the ceiling, ducts or fittings, but also its material character as defined by the materials and the construction method.

A perception of the physical presence of space and the structural qualities that define it is of primary importance for understanding how space is formed. It provides us with the basis from which to elaborate spatial qualities in the service of an overall idea. Similarly, a better awareness of the consequences of design decisions affords us new possibilities for aesthetic experimentation and reveals the cubature potential encompassed within a simple container of space.

The Best Room project is an exploration of the ideal qualities of space. It examines not just its floor-plan relations and its sculptural appearance, but also how it reflects the everyday activities that take place within in it in such a way that the use of a space becomes an architectural experience.

---

1 "Hope", verse 5439, Johann Wolfgang von Goethe, Faust: *The Second Part of the Tragedy*, trans. and intro. David Constantine (London: Penguin, 2009).

2 Henri Lefebvre, *The Production of Space*, trans. Donald Nicholson-Smith (Oxford: Basil Blackwell, 1991), p. 15.

3 August Schmarsow, *Das Wesen der architektonischen Schöpfung* (Leipzig: Hiersemann, 1894), published in English version under the title *The Essence of Architectural Creation*.

4 Geoffrey Scott, *The Architecture of Humanism: A Study in the History of Taste* (Boston, MA, New York: Houghton Mifflin, 1914), p. 226.

5 Albert Erich Brinckmann, *Plastik und Raum als Grundformen künstlerischer Gestaltung* (Munich: Piper Verlag, 1922).

6 Luigi Moretti, "Strutture e sequenze di spazi", *Spazio* IV, 7 (December 1952–April 1953), pp. 9–20 and 107–8. Translated as "Structures and Sequences of Spaces", in Federico Bucci and Marco Mulazzani, *Luigi Moretti: Works and Writings* (New York: Princeton Architectural Press, 2002), pp. 177–82.

Candice Baldy

Scale 1:200

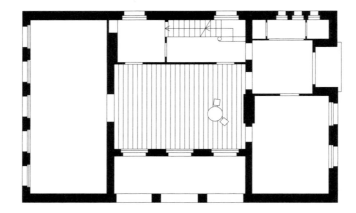

164 Ludwig Mies van der Rohe, Hugo Perls House, Berlin, 1912 The Best Room Laboratory EAST

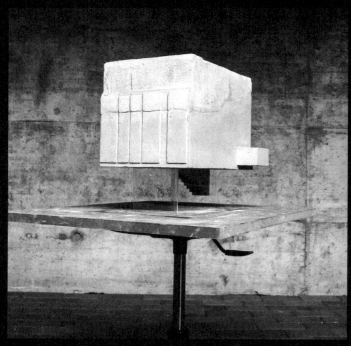

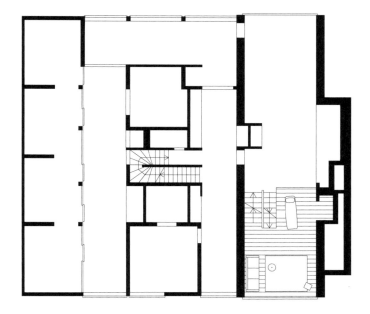

Marlon Biétry

Scale 1:300

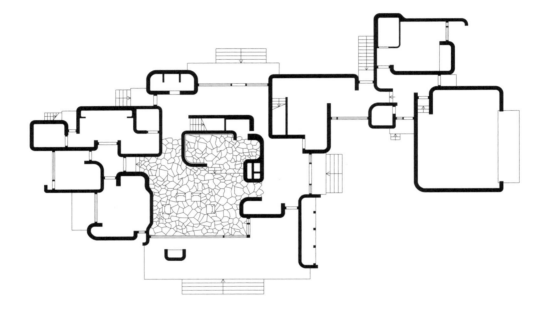

168 John M. Johansen, Labyrinth House, Southport, Connecticut, 1966   The Best Room   Laboratory EAST

Scale 1:200 Félix Caspary

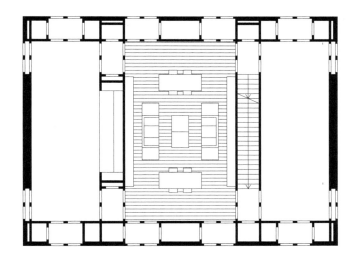

Laboratory EAST   The Best Room   Oswald Mathias Ungers, House Without Qualities, Cologne, 1996   171

Gabriel Chareton

Scale 1:500

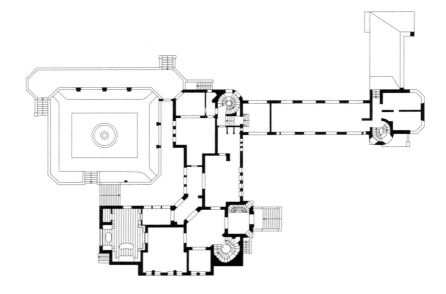

172 Henri van der Velde, Villa Hohenhof, Hohenhof, 1908 The Best Room Laboratory EAST

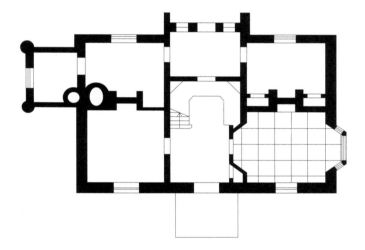

Léonard Darbellay

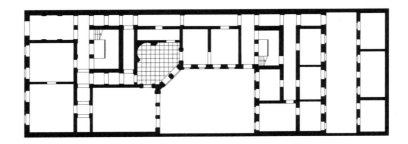

176   Karl Friedrich Schinkel, town house, Potsdam, 1829   The Best Room   Laboratory EAST

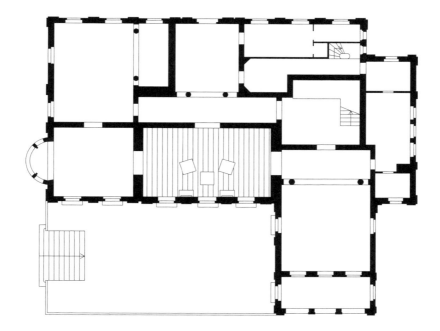

Gabriel Disner

Scale 1:200

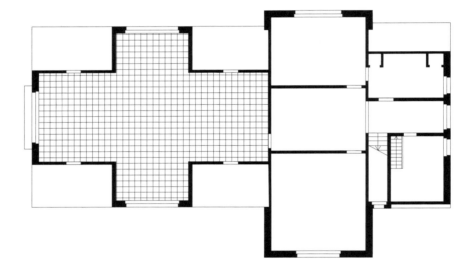

180   Lux Guyer, Villa Boverie, Zurich, 1932   The Best Room   Laboratory EAST

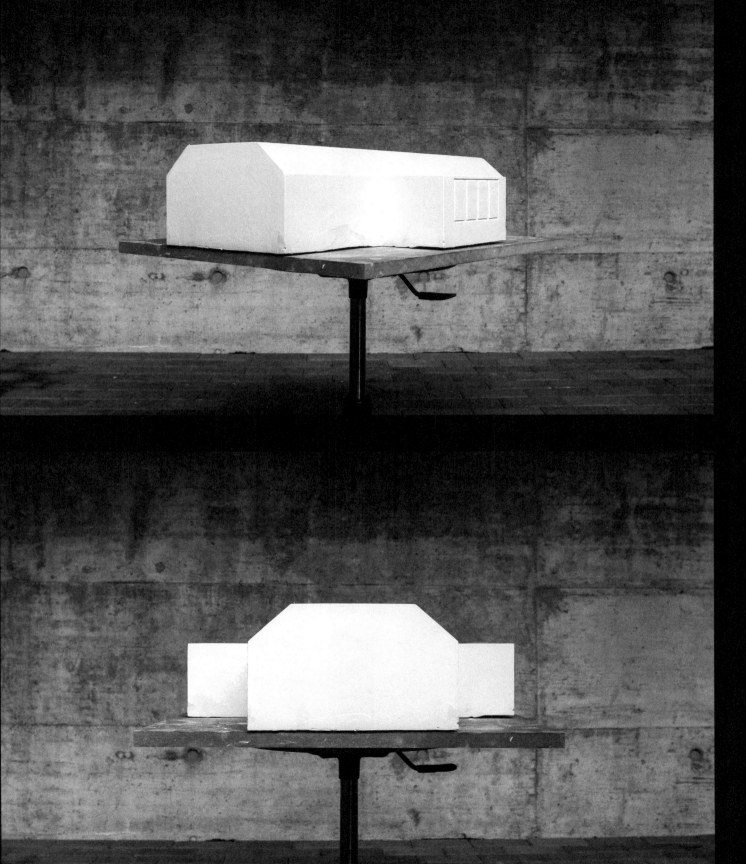

Scale 1:200 Christopher El Hayek

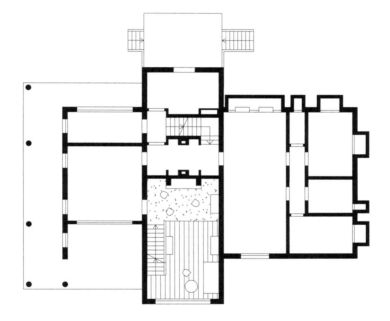

Laboratory EAST   The Best Room   Lux Guyer, Sunnebüel House, Küsnacht, 1930

Marc Evéquoz

Scale 1:200

184 Adolf Loos, Müller House, Prague, 1930 The Best Room Laboratory EAST

Scale 1:300 Sami Farra

Laboratory EAST | The Best Room | Rudolph Michael Schindler, Schindler Chase House, Hollywood, California, 1922

Léa Gauchoux

Scale 1:500

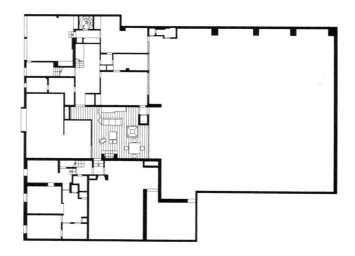

188 Luis Barragán, House Barragán, Mexico City, 1948 The Best Room Laboratory EAST

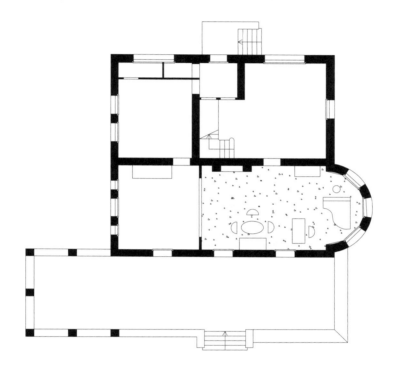

Charles Jenny

Scale 1:500

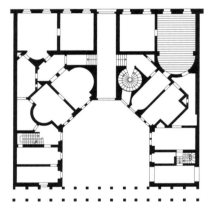

192   Karl Friedrich Schinkel, Feilner House, Berlin, 1829   The Best Room   Laboratory EAST

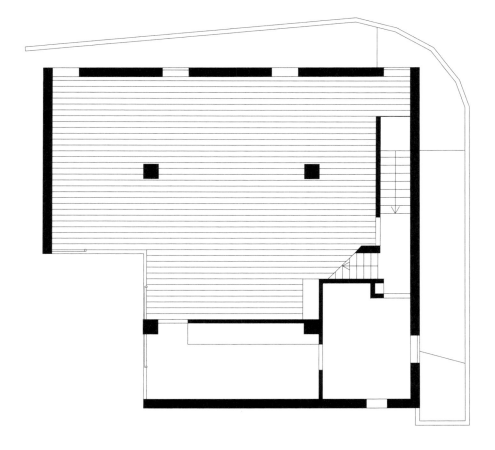

Gentian Kadrijaj

Scale 1:500

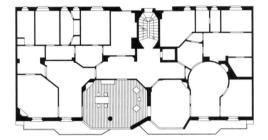

196 — Luigi Caccia Dominioni, apartment building on via G. Vigoni, Milan, 1959 — The Best Room — Laboratory EAST

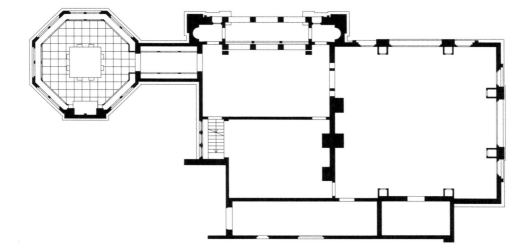

Théophile Legrain

Scale 1:500

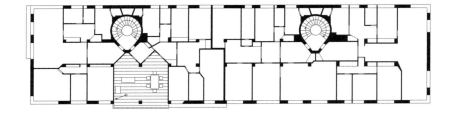

200 — Luigi Caccia Dominioni, housing block on via Ippolito Nievo, Milan, 1957 — The Best Room — Laboratory EAST

Scale 1:1000

Alexandra Liebich

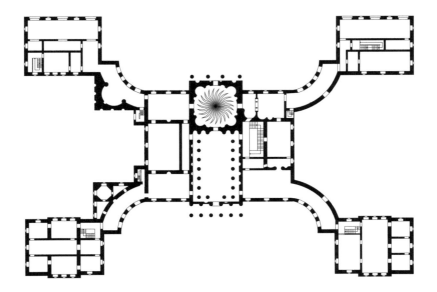

Laboratory EAST   The Best Room   Robert Adam, Kedleston Hall, Derbyshire, 1770

203

Afroditi Maloukotsi

Scale 1:200

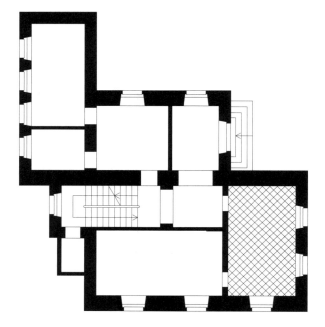

204 — Gottfried Semper, Villa Garbald, Castasegna, 1864 — The Best Room — Laboratory EAST

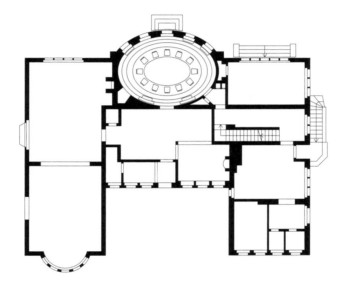

Justine Rausis

Scale 1:200

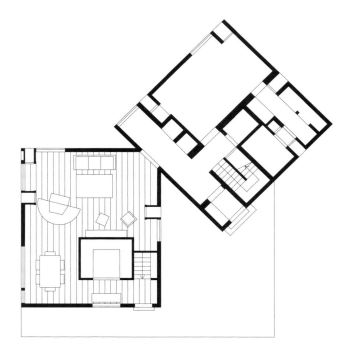

208 — Louis Kahn, Fisher House, Hatboro, Pennsylvania, 1967 — The Best Room — Laboratory EAST

Scale 1:300

Valentin Rey

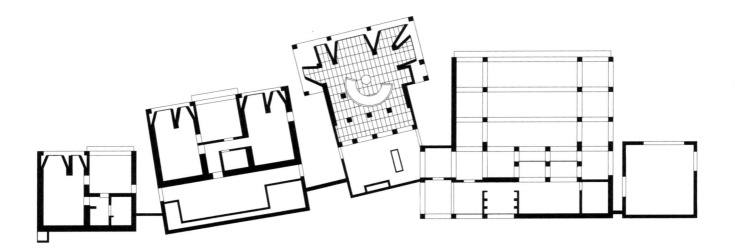

Laboratory EAST The Best Room Jørn Utzon, Can Lis, Mallorca, 1973 **211**

Marc Reymond

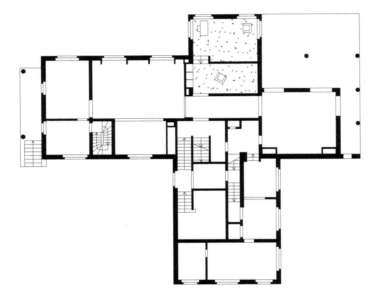

212   Lux Guyer, Rudolph House, Küsnacht, 1931   The Best Room   Laboratory EAST

Scale 1:200 David Richner

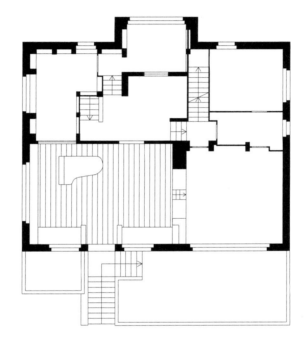

Laboratory EAST   The Best Room   Adolf Loos, Moller House, Vienna, 1928

Margaux Ruiz

Scale 1:300

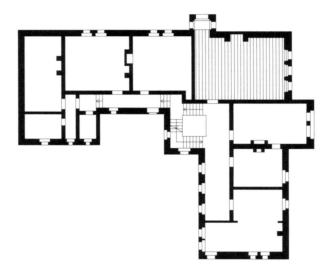

216 Philip Webb, Red House, Bexleyheath, 1859 The Best Room Laboratory EAST

Scale 1:200

Diane Stierli

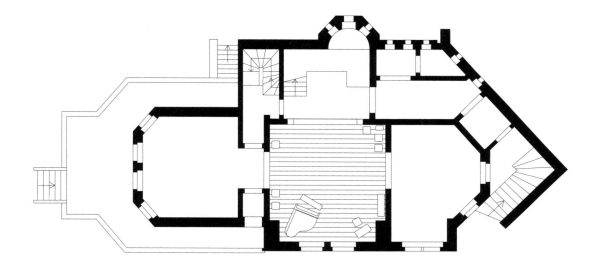

Laboratory EAST   The Best Room   Henri van der Velde, Hohe Pappeln House, Weimar, 1908

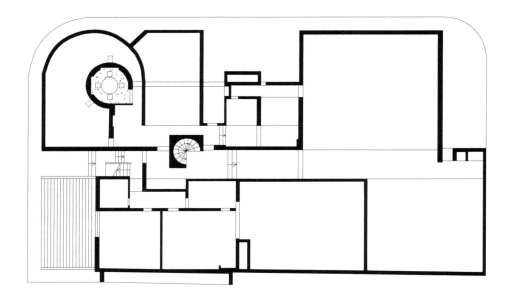

Scale 1:300

Romain Thiébaud

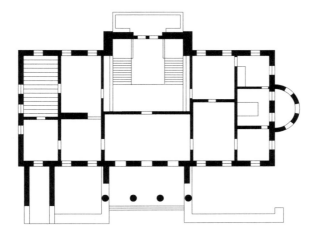

Laboratory EAST The Best Room Karl Friedrich Schinkel, Tent Room, Charlottenhof Palace, Potsdam, 1829

Marc Vertesi

Scale 1:200

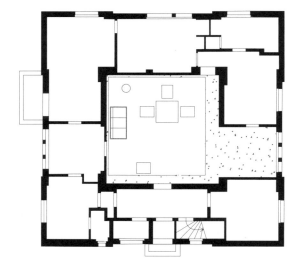

224 — Georg Muche, model house Am Horn, Weimar, 1923 — The Best Room — Laboratory EAST

Scale 1:300

Teo Vexina Wilkinson

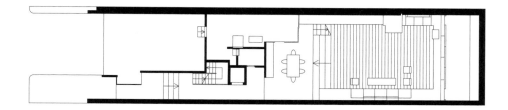

Laboratory EAST The Best Room Paul Rudolph, Hirsch House, New York, 1967 **227**

Killian Worreth

Scale 1:300

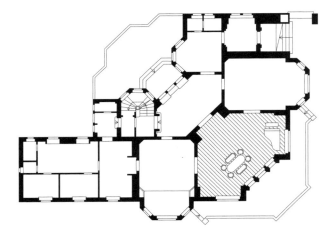

228   Thilo Schoder, Lessner House, Weimar, 1923   The Best Room   Laboratory EAST

Ursina Ziörjen

Scale 1:300

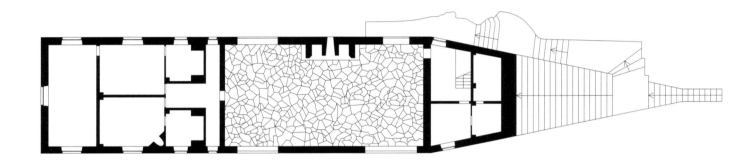

232 Curzio Malaparte, Villa Malaparte, Capri, 1942 The Best Room Laboratory EAST

The Art of Seeing: The Still Image

Anja & Martin Fröhlich

Perceiving space – representing space

When we stand in a room, we cannot take all of it in at once. What we perceive is a series of individual impressions, each of them incomplete. Even a simple volume, such as a room, cannot be comprehended in its entirety; all we see is part of the walls, some corners, windows or a ceiling. The same applies when we represent a space. Here too we can only depict a fragment of the space or a single directional view within it.

Various strategies have been developed to get over this limitation and to expand or extend the depiction of a space. One approach, employed by the painters of church interiors, was to portray several views in different directions, the painter Jacobus Balthasar Peeters, for example, producing several paintings of the interior of the Carolus Borromeuskerk in Antwerp (c.1730). To reveal parts of interiors not visible from the viewer's standpoint, it was also common practice to incorporate a mirror into the painting to extend the perception of space, one of the first paintings to employ this device being Jan van Eyck's *The Arnolfini Portrait* (1434). The mirror shows not only the reflected rearward view of the scene in the painting but also the articulation of the space behind the viewer.

But a picture always has an end, an edge and often also a frame. It shows only a part, a vignette, of the reality it portrays. While our visual perception of space likewise only affords us a partial view of the real world, it is not as sharply delineated as that of a picture. Our visual field becomes more blurred and less coloured towards its edges. In addition, we can seamlessly extend our visual field to the left and right or up and down. To portray how we see in the real world on a flat canvas, painting has traditionally used perspective as a geometric instrument. Much like in an architectural drawing, the viewer is drawn into the illusion of an architectural scene through the device of an idealised view of an object within it. The perspective directs our gaze to a specific viewpoint at a particular position.

In the painted ceilings of the Baroque, the architecture of the building and the three-dimensionality of the rich mouldings around the pictures were conceived from the outset not just as a device for framing the paintings but as part of the overall composition. Spaces with colossal painted ceilings were frequently devised to be viewed from specific vantages. Sometimes it seems as if entire interiors were designed around the optimal viewpoints from which to observe the paintings. One such example is Andrea Pozzo's ceiling fresco *Glorification of Saint Ignatius* (1691–4) in the nave of the church of Sant'Ignazio in Rome, in which a marble panel in the floor denotes the ideal standpoint from which to view the frescoes above.

Perspective and the art of optical illusion

The process of seeing and the transmission of light was described by the French philosopher and mathematician René Descartes using the metaphor of a person crossing uneven ground at night, or a blind man tapping out a path between obstacles using a cane or walking stick.[1] The essence of seeing and portraying in perspective is based on the simple model of a cone of rays of light. Objects within the visual field of the eye are seen well-defined, as if illuminated by a searchlight. Everything outside this cone is shrouded in darkness, and as such is unrecognisable.

Filippo Brunelleschi employed this principle when locating his first central perspective – that of the Baptistery of Saint John in Florence (1425) – at a specific point within the Cattedrale di Santa Maria del Fiore: the portal constrained the visual field on all sides so that the painting needed only depict the part of the piazza that the eye can see. The device of perspective delineates a space beyond which there is only the invisible material of the "outside world". Architectural perspective was developed to simulate the sense of depth of our natural field of vision: the viewpoint and direction are strategically chosen so that the impression of the buildings looks realistic when seen from that specific fixed point. Consequently, such depictions have a calculated perspective effect. However, not all perspectives can be translated into three-dimensional reality.

Nevertheless, the convincing realism of representations using perspective is not immune to manipulation. Small optical adjustments in scale, for example, can create a more generous impression of space than the floor plan actually affords. In perspective view, the difference between architecture and an image can appear negligible. The obvious three-dimensionality of buildings and the fact that, due to the various mathematical rules it adheres to, architecture is frequently rectilinear means that it has always served both as a model for demonstrating the geometric principles of perspective as well as a field for experimenting with it.

What works convincingly in a painting cannot always be translated into real architecture. Conversely, some architects have also attempted to create an architectural impression in three dimensions that deceives the viewer when seen from a certain viewpoint. What in reality is a bas-relief appears to the eye as a deep altar niche. Similarly, a series of successively smaller columns can create a perceived impression of depth that does not exist in reality, allowing the sculpture at the end to appear larger than it really is. Francesco Borromini's perspective device of illusory depth in his corridor at Palazzo Spada in Rome (c.1635) employs the same principles as Vincenzo Scarmozzi's stage sets in Andrea Palladio's Teatro Olimpico (1585) in Vicenza. In the latter case, to heighten the impression of depth, the floor of the stage rises towards the rear while the size of the buildings depicted in the street-scenes decreases. The result is that although the stage is 12 metres deep, an impression is created of streets that recede hundreds of metres into the distance.

Space as image – image as space

In Vicenza, the correspondence of painted and architectural illusion is seamless. When such effects are incorporated into real architecture, they reveal something that is normally not so apparent, namely that architecture is frequently perceived in terms of images or successions of images. Correspondingly, our sense of a space becomes a measure of the amount of time the viewer needs to pass through it. In such cases, shifts in perspective, whether orchestrated or by chance, become increasingly important. Moments of surprise arise when such an image acts to halt this flow and itself becomes the dominant impression, as is the case with Borromini's corridor. One becomes aware of the perspective view as a moment "frozen in time", and for one brief instance the artifice of the perspective impression matches our sense of vision.

Throughout the ages, optical illusions have been a favourite device in paintings, and for some it was the very purpose of perspective construction. Among the advocates of this school of thought, Johann Heinrich Lambert is perhaps the most well known. The mathematician wrote several important treatises on the subject of perspective, remarking on its purpose as follows: "Vision is concerned with the mechanics of how we differentiate the appearance of things from their true form, and how we recognise them by their appearance. Perspective is less concerned with true form than with conveying an apparent form. The more exacting a painting is, the more convincing the illusion. The ultimate accomplishment is that a painting succeeds in completely deceiving the eye."[2] What Lambert differentiates between here is vision, which aims to decipher the true form behind the appearance of things, and perspective, whose ultimate aim he saw as being able to faithfully mislead the human gaze.

One of the most convincing proponents of the art of optical illusion is M.C. Escher, who experimented extensively with how we see and perceive things, employing the means of perspective to create new images that cause us to question what we see. His impossible but nonetheless still conceivable perspectives portray plausible-looking spaces that defy actual construction in three dimensions.[3]

To summarise, our perception is grounded not solely on a theory of what we see in terms of image but also on the visual method of constructing images as a means of creating objects. In the process of shaping images on a two-dimensional medium, the spaces they portray are *per se* an optical illusion – one in which three-dimensional objects are represented on a two-dimensional surface in such a way that they produce an impression of space.

The art of composing and perceiving perspective impressions is ultimately determined by a dual set of underlying circumstances: firstly, the question of how much more background information the horizon of a composition reveals compared to what it shows; and, secondly, how rapidly the still appearance of the composed image is lost in the flow of space and impressions around it.

1   René Descartes, *Dioptrik*, trans. and ed. Gertrud Leisegang (Meisenheim am Glan: Westkulturverlag Anton Hain, 1954), pp. 69–70; S.Y. Edgerton, Jr., *The Renaissance Rediscovery of Linear Perspective* (New York: Basic Books, 1975), pp. 100–2.

2   Johann Heinrich Lambert, *Die freye Perspektive* (Zurich, 1759 and 1774), cited in J. H. Lambert, *Schriften zur Perspektive*, ed. Max Steck (Berlin: Georg Lüttke Verlag, 1943), p. 263.

3   J. L. Locher (ed.), *Die Welten des M.C. Escher* (Munich: Manfred Pawlak Verlagsgesellschaft, 1971); Bruno Ernst, *Der Zauberspiegel des M.C. Escher* (Munich: Verlag Heinz Moos, 1978).

Scale 1:200

Antoine Béguin

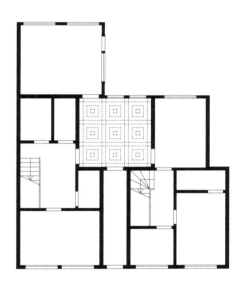

Laboratory EAST   The Best Room   Pieter Janssens Elinga, *Interior with Painter (...)*, c.1665–1670   **239**

Marlon Biétry

Scale 1:200

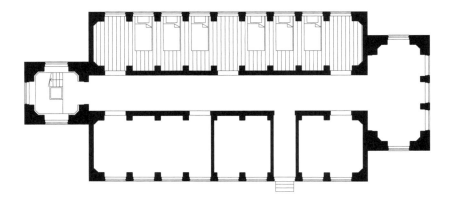

240 James Tissot, *Green Room of Comédie-Français During the Seige of Paris*, 1877 The Best Room Laboratory EAST

Scale 1:500

Andrei Rjabuschkin

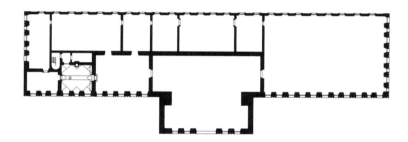

Laboratory EAST The Best Room Andrei Rjabuschkin, *Red House*, 1899 **243**

Léonard Darbelltay

Scale 1:200

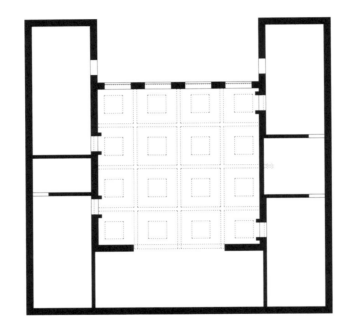

244 Konstantin Korovin, *Summer Study of Prince Vasily Golitsyn*, 1911   The Best Room   Laboratory EAST

Scale 1:200

Sophie Di Rosa

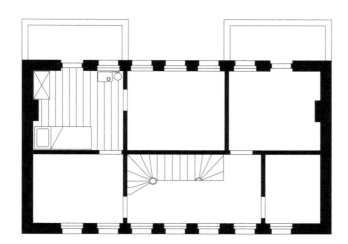

Laboratory EAST   The Best Room   Konstantin Somov, *The interior*. Second part, 1934   **247**

Gabriel Disner

Scale 1:500

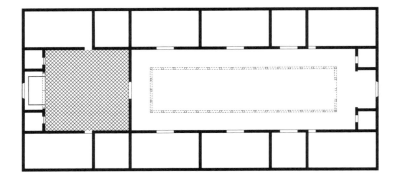

248 Eugene Delacroix, *Intérieur mauresque (...)*, 1832   The Best Room   Laboratory EAST

Scale 1:200
Christopher El Hayek

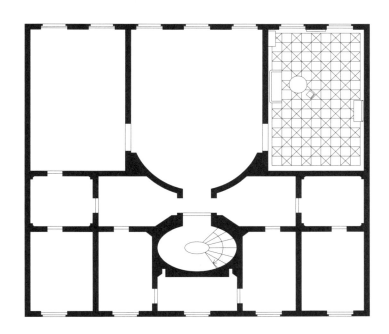

Laboratory EAST   The Best Room   Johann Erdmann Hummel, *Interior with Three Mirrors*, c.1820   **251**

Marc Evéquoz

Scale 1:200

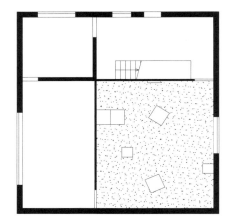

252 Winston Churchill, *Room at Breccles*, Norfolk, 1920 The Best Room Laboratory EAST

Scale 1:200   Sami Farra

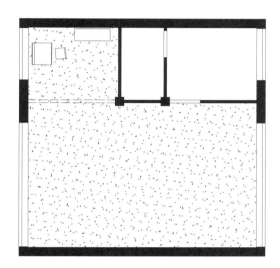

Laboratory EAST   The Best Room   Carl Larsson, *Esbjorn Doing His Homework*, 1912   255

Léa Gauchoux

Scale 1:200

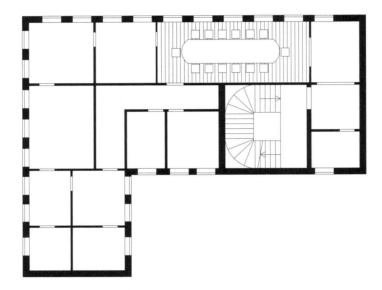

256   Vilhelm Hammershøi, *Interior, Frederiksberg Allé*, c.1900   The Best Room   Laboratory EAST

Scale 1:100

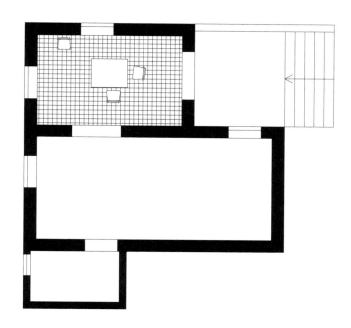

Juliette Jancu

Laboratory EAST   The Best Room   John Miller, *The Yellow Chair*, n.d.

Charles Jenny

Scale 1:500

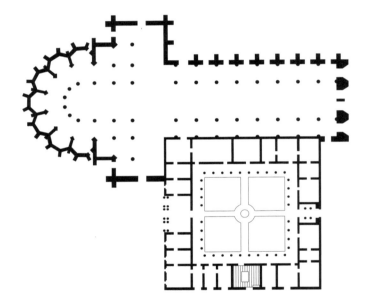

260 Lucas Cranach the Elder, *Cardinal Albrecht of Brandenburg (...)*, 1525 The Best Room Laboratory EAST

Scale 1:500

Gentian Kadrijaj

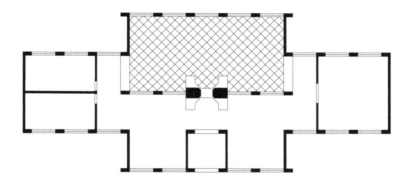

Laboratory EAST　　　The Best Room　　　Johannes Vermeer, *A Lady at the Virginals with a Gentleman*, c.1662–5

263

Théophile Legrain

Scale 1:200

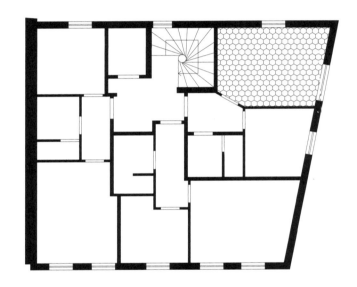

264 Gwen John, *A Corner of the Artist's Room in Paris*, 1907–9   The Best Room   Laboratory EAST

Scale 1:100   Afroditi Maloukotsi

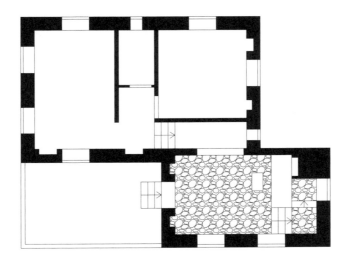

Laboratory EAST   The Best Room   Georg Friedrich Kersting, *Woman Embroidering*, 1812   **267**

Justine Rausis

Scale 1:200

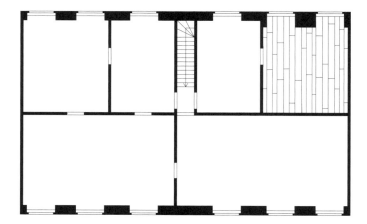

268   Caspar David Friedrich, *Woman at the Window*, 1822   The Best Room   Laboratory EAST

Scale 1:200 — David Richner

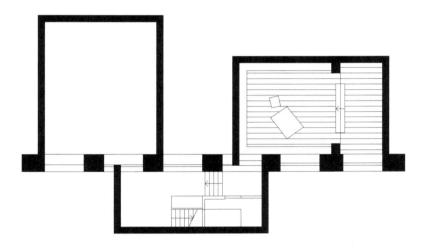

Laboratory EAST   The Best Room   Albrecht Dürer, *St Jerome in His Study*, 1514   271

Margaux Ruiz

Scale 1:100

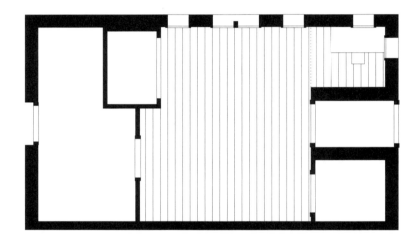

272 Pieter de Hooch, *A Mother Delousing Her Child's Hair*, c.1658–60　　The Best Room　　Laboratory EAST

Scale 1:100

Diane Stierli

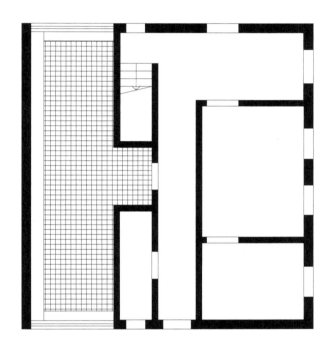

Laboratory EAST   The Best Room   Grant Wood, *The sun shine on the corner*, 1928   **275**

Romain Thiébaud

Scale 1:500

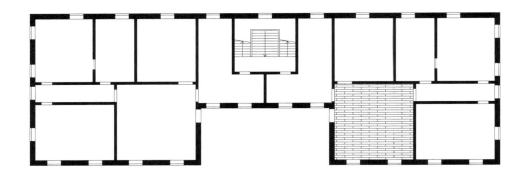

276 Vilhelm Hammershøi, *Interior in Strandgade, Sunlight on the Floor*, 1901 The Best Room Laboratory EAST

Scale 1:200 Teo Vexina Wilkinson

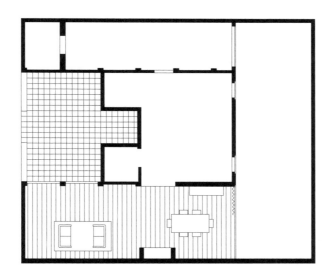

Laboratory EAST The Best Room Lawrence Alma-Tadema, *Interior of Caius Martius' House*, 1901

Killian Worreth

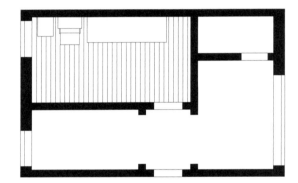

280 Adolph Menzel, *Das Schlafzimmer des Künstlers in der Ritterstraße*, 1847   The Best Room   Laboratory EAST

Scale 1:200   Marine Wyssbrod

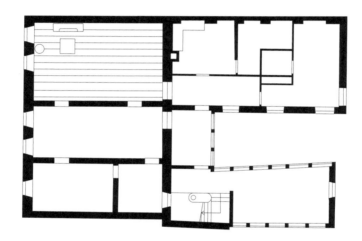

Laboratory EAST   The Best Room   Vilhelm Hammershøi, *Interieur, Strandgade 30*, 1900   **283**

A Brief History of the Living Room

Marie Theres Stauffer

The following deliberations concern the living room – what is called in French the *salon* and in German the *Wohnzimmer*. Today, the living room is conventionally the "best room" within a house or apartment. It is both the centre of social interactions as well as the culmination of the residents' representational aspirations. In history, however, the living room has changed over the centuries as a spatial typology. In this particular case our thoughts concern some historical instances of the living room as it developed in France. This cultural–geographical focus has been chosen because the architecture of the nobility in France in the early modern period gave rise to a specific distribution of living rooms, which over the centuries spread throughout Europe and in certain respects has survived on into the twenty-first century. It is not by chance that the architecture and living arrangements of this particular social group is of relevance: the aristocracy were particularly given to arranging social occasions and to holding these within suitably representative settings.[1] Over time, the spatial concepts of the *noblesse* came to serve as a model for the bourgeoisie that in certain aspects continues to hold true to the present day.

In the history of French interiors, the *salon* originates from the medieval *salle* or hall. As one of the most generously proportioned rooms in a house, it was accorded greater status than the other rooms and was large enough to serve many uses: on the one hand, it was a place for concerts, celebrations, games and banquets; and on the other, a space for teaching children or a place for several people to sleep when the house was full.[2]

By the late fifteenth to, early sixteenth century, the hall, while still a reception room, was no longer the most prestigious room in the house. Guests of sufficient status were received, often as a select group, in the *chambre de parade*: this room served both as a reception room and as a living room, set apart together with the cabinet room beyond it, but still in direct relationship to the *salle*. Sometimes it directly adjoined the *salle* [Fig. 1]; sometimes it was located on the other side of a vestibule from which the other representative rooms were accessed [Fig. 2].[3] The *chambre de parade* was usually reached via at least one *antichambre*. Persons of lower rank did not progress any further than this anteroom. Behind the *chambre de parade* were one or more cabinet rooms, which were small, introverted spaces. As a rule, each successive space was more lavishly decorated than the next, culminating in the first instance in the *chambre de parade*. The cabinet rooms beyond were no less important, but related directly to the *chambre*: only guests of high rank were granted access to the *chambre*, and of those only a few were able to progress onwards into the truly exclusive sphere beyond.[4]

In the *appartement* of the sixteenth and seventeenth centuries, we can see the same typological elements of the *salle*, *chambre* and *cabinet*, likewise arranged as a succession of representative spaces in the living areas of the town houses or castles of the nobility [Fig. 3].[5] The resulting impression of a progression of spaces could be heightened by arranging these rooms in linear succession beyond one another and connecting them with likewise axially arranged connecting doors *en enfilade* [Fig. 4]. This configuration, which afforded guests a glimpse of the entire succession of spaces through the consecutive sequence of openings, became established around 1630.[6] The differently appointed rooms, each with its own symbolic capital, made it possible to separate off and thus distinguish prestigious occasions, whereby – as befitting their social status – visitors could be received in what was the best (possible) room.

Towards the end of the seventeenth century, and subsequently over the course of the eighteenth century, the *salle* became gradually replaced by a smaller *salon* [Fig. 5]. During the same period, the living rooms were increasingly accorded specific functions. In the process, the *chambre* gradually became less and less important for representative occasions and increasingly a space of retreat, with social life instead shifting back towards the *salon*. This corresponds, more or less, to what we now know as the "best room" of the modern age.

To come full circle, and by taking a renewed look at current living arrangements, we can observe that living rooms with specific and distinct functions are in fact a convention of the recent past that currently, or indeed still, predominate – a prevalence that surprisingly remains regardless of more recent experiments with multifunctional spaces. A representative example of the "best room" from the age of so-called high modernism might be the reception room in Villa Shodan in Ahmedabad, designed by Le Corbusier between 1951 and 1956 [Fig. 6].[7] While the space of the *salon* flows on into the garden and other spaces on the ground floor, it has a largely prescribed structural purpose. What the example demonstrates is that an impressive representative status and prestigious architecture was of similar importance to the Indian industrialists of the modern age, and their architect, as it was for the *noblesse* of the past, thus representing a perceptible continuity to the *appartements de parade* of the early modern period.

---

1   See in particular Norbert Elias, *Die höfische Gesellschaft: Untersuchungen zur Soziologie des Königtums und der höfischen Aristokratie* (Frankfurt a.M.: Suhrkamp, 1983); Peter Thornton, *Authentic Decor: The Domestic Interior 1620–1920* (London: Seven Dials, 2000); Peter Thornton, *Seventeenth-Century Interior Decoration in England, France and Holland* (New Haven: Yale University Press, 1990); Jean Feray, *Architecture intérieure et décoration en France des origines à 1875* (Paris: Berger-Levrault Caisse nationale des monuments historiques et des sites, 1988).

2   See Jean-Pierre Babelon, *Demeures parisiennes sous Henri IV et Louis XIII* (Paris: Hazan, 1991); Wolfram Prinz and Ronald G. Kecks, *Das französische Schloss der Renaissance: Form und Bedeutung der Architektur, ihre geschichtlichen und gesellschaftlichen Grundlagen* (Berlin: Verlag Gebrüder Mann, 1985), pp. 129–31; Jean-Marie Pérouse de Montclos, *Architecture: Méthode et vocabulaire* (Paris: Impr. nationale, 1972), p. 229.

3   Prinz an Kecks, *Das französische Schloss*, p. 130; Pérouse de Montclos, *Architecture*, p. 229.

4   See for example Alain Mérot, *Retraites mondaines: Aspects de la décoration intérieure à Paris, au XVIIe siècle* (Paris: Le Promeneur, 1990), pp. 12–19; Pérouse de Montclos, *Architecture*, p. 229. See also the term "cabinet" in Edmond Huguet, *Dictionnaire de la langue française du seizième siècle*, vol. 2 (Paris: Champion, 1932); the term "cabinet" in Denis Diderot and Jean le Rond d'Alembert, *Encyclopédie, ou Dictionnaire raisonné des sciences, des arts et des métiers* (Paris: Briasson, 1751).

5   Prinz an Kecks, *Das französische Schloss*, p. 130.

6   Thornton, *Authentic Decor*, p. 63; Feray, *Architecture intérieure*, pp. 61–2 and 96–102.

7   For the most recent publication on the subject see Eric Touchaleaume and Gérald Moreau, *Le Corbusier, Pierre Jeanneret: L'aventure indienne / The Indian Adventure – Design, Art, Architecture* (Montreuil: Gourcuff Gradenigo, 2010).

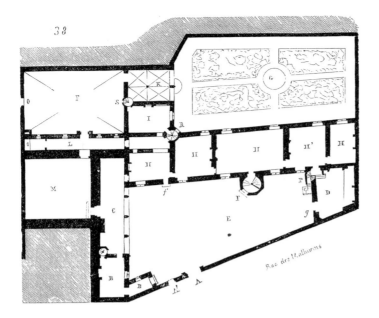

[Fig. 1]
Architect unknown, Hôtel Cluny, Paris, c.1471–1500. Hypothetical reconstruction of the ground floor of the house. The *salle* is located in the centre of the main wing between the court and the garden; it is entered via the vestibule in the staircase. The *chambre de parade* and *cabinet* probably led off from one side of the *salle*.

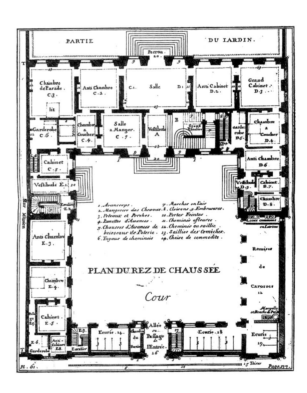

[Fig. 3]
Augustins-Charles d'Avilers, model design for a town house. Ground-floor plan, published in *Cours d'architecture* (Paris: Nicolas Langlois, 1691). The *salle* is arranged on the central axis of the main wing and is reached via a vestibule. The *chambre de parade* is arranged left of the *salle*, the other representative rooms to the right of it.

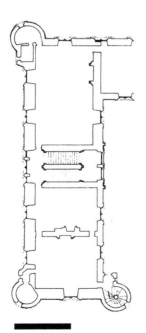

[Fig. 2]
Architect unknown, Castle Azay-le-Rideau, Azay-le-Rideau, 1518–27. The *salle* is separated from the *chambre de parade* and *cabinet* by the vestibule and stair.

[Fig. 4]
Charles Chamois, and others, Hôtel de Lauzun, Paris. Interiors from the 1660s: view down the enfilade of *parade appartements* on the second floor.

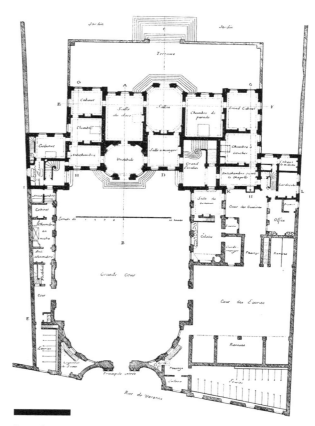

[Fig. 5]
Jean Courtonne and Antoine Mazin, Hôtel de Matignon, Paris, 1722–4, ground-floor plan, published in Jacques-François Blondel, *Architecture Françoise*, vol. 1 (Paris: Charles-Antoine Jombert, 1752). Behind the vestibule is a throne room, to the right of it the reception rooms with *salon*, *chambre de parade* and *grand cabinet*.

[Fig. 6]
Le Corbusier, Villa Shodan, Ahmedabad, 1952–6. *Salon* on the ground floor.

Inaugurated in 1927, the cabin of A Neuve reflects the turbulent history of alpinism in the Canton of Valais. At the time it was built, it was highly popular with Alpinists, but as a result of the surrounding Alpine routes having partially lost their attractiveness the cabin is now facing a decline in attendance. The Swiss Alpine Club asked design studio EAST to tackle this challenge by designing an extension to the cabin, with the aim of developing a new and appealing programme. Two prototypes were built and temporary installed in the region over the course of a year. One of the prototypes is now in the process of being developed to be reproduced and installed around the area of the A Neuve hut at La Fouly.

A Neuve Twin Pavilions

Photographs
Joël Tettamanti

2017

Modern Times

2015

The research design studio focused on the programmatic and spatial reorganisation of the area housing the headquarters of the leading retailing company Migros in Zurich-West. The main goal of the research studio was to address the issue of complex planning and programmatic reorganisation in dealing with a structure almost the size of an entire neighbourhood. In order to develop a consistent architectural project, the students were challenged to work with different degrees of precision, scales and atmospheres, ranging from large public spaces to intimate private ones.

The goal of the design and research studio Modern Times was to test programmatic and — ultimately — economic models that could prove robust enough to inscribe a company's ambition into the energetic development of a city like Zurich.

The Pursuit of Happiness

Tiago P. Borges

"A story of industry, of individual enterprise — humanity crusading in the pursuit of happiness."[1] This is the sentence that opens *Modern Times*, a silent (or almost silent) movie directed by Charlie Chaplin in 1936. In it, Chaplin illustrates the impact of the Great Depression in the eyes of his iconic character the Little Tramp, a nut-tightener working for the Electro Steel Corporation. The plot of the movie revolves around the progression of his misadventures as he fights to make a living and to reconcile himself to modern times. Midway through the film, the Electro Steel Corp is forced to close, leaving its entire workforce out of work. In his character's vain anticipation of prosperity, Chaplin aptly captures the soul of the city and its industrial architecture as similarly unemployed — receptacles of glass, concrete and stone, victim to the same arbitrariness of economic incertitude. Taking this theme as its motto, the eponymous design studio Modern Times pursued an interest in the large industrial and logistics infrastructures left abandoned and desolate by the same force of relentless rationalisation.

The Swiss Migros company, founded by Gottlieb Duttweiler in 1925, has progressed from its humble beginnings to become what now is the country's largest retailer. In Zurich, the focus of Migros's growth was the Escher Wyss district, where the company's logistics centre is located and where for many years it dominated the area's urban development. More recently, the entire sector along Pfingstweidstrasse has been subject to significant changes, led by the transformation of the Toni-Areal site. Due to the modernisation, several parts of Migros's centre became obsolete, and thus vacant, prompting the company to issue a call for new programmatic proposals to boost its presence and to also enable it to actively contribute to the overall municipal strategic vision for the district. In addition, Migros's vision was to create a public hub, based on a marketplace typology and offering a mixed scenario for gastronomy, retail, culture, education and recreation within a ten-year time frame.

The sheer dimensions of the site of the headquarters — more than 150,000 square metres of gross floor area — enabled the studio to embrace the issue of "bigness", as articulated by Rem Koolhaas/OMA: "But in fact only Bigness instigates the regime of complexity that mobilizes the full intelligence of architecture and its related fields."[2] Following this structure, the studio chose to loosen the existing building infrastructure and pre-existing programmatic constraints by injecting a complexity factor, which simultaneously needed to be a continual given during the construction phase itself. This principle, coupled with the context, had the advantage of allowing the studio to synchronously continue its ongoing research into hybrid programmes. As set, the programme stipulated shared facilities and a 24/7 use cycle, the goal therefore being to transcend standard mixed-used models. The client's remit was that the project have the potential to fully embrace innovative scenarios in order to create a new kind of cultural institution. In response, the Modern Times studio formulated a wide range of approaches: not only overall concepts, but simultaneously key-point projects establishing multiple degrees of precision, scales and atmospheres, ranging from large public areas to more intimate ones.

A general starting point was established through preliminary group research, forming a basis for three main trajectories: logistics, organisation, programme and typologies, and urban composition. Ostensibly, the Modern Times studio implemented a series of dynamic inputs formulated out of the tension between the existing and proposed programmes. However, beyond their articulation in technical drawings, these projects were in reality presented in "silent" images, in other words devoid of any traces of the daily life of their inhabitants. The only item that assists the observer to build his or her own narrative of the project is the insertion of discrete signs—a deliberate contradiction that urges the reader to focus on the architecture, on the elements that delimit the spaces and that give them their qualities, or for that matter flaws. In presentational terms, the projects were complemented by a sole exterior image, intended to assist a better recognition of the interventions and transformations deployed. Although single, not multiple, this image performs an essential role in underlining the urban presence of each proposal in what is a post-industrial landscape, which in planning terms is achievable either through the strength of the built volumes or alternatively by the spacious voids that underscore their very absence. The goal of this design and research studio was to test programmatic and—ultimately—economic models that could prove robust enough to inscribe a company's ambition into the energetic development of a city like Zurich. With this set of scenarios, the students were able to develop an understanding of how challenging "modern times" can be, and that only by adopting an innate optimism —with the Little Tramp's adventure in mind—can one indeed find ways to keep "crusading in the pursuit of happiness" in architecture.

1 Charlie Chaplin (dir.), *Modern Times* (1936), YouTube, https://bit.ly/2utS5RD (last accessed 1 July 2018).

2 Rem Koolhaas, "Bigness (or the problem of the large)", in Rem Koolhaas and Bruce Mau, *S,M,L,XL: O.M.A.* (New York: Monacelli Press, 1995), pp. 494–516, here p. 494. S,M,L,XL: Small, medium, large, extra-large.

Scale 1:2500

Adrien Liaudat & Lerna Bagdjian

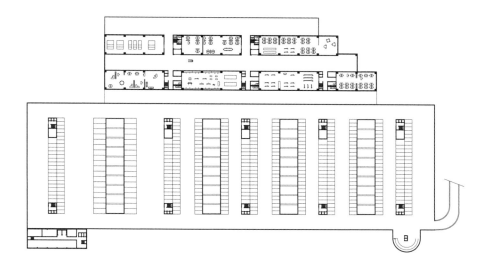

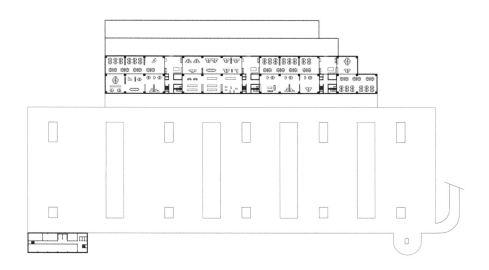

Laboratory EAST   Modern Times   Souk   **305**

Amelia Baldie & Anne Choukroun

Scale 1:2500

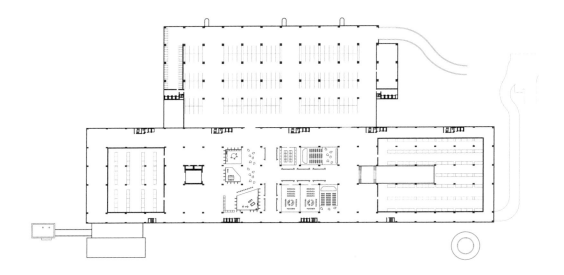

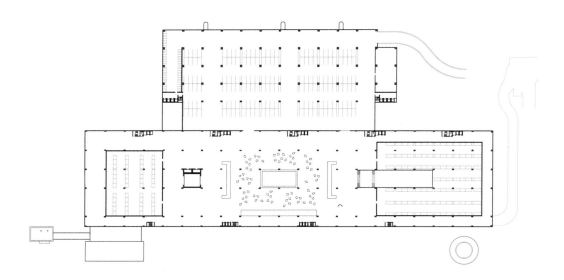

306   Kubrik   Modern Times   Laboratory EAST

Scale 1:2500

Francesco Anfosso & Laura Bornet

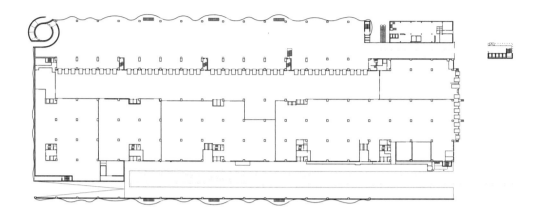

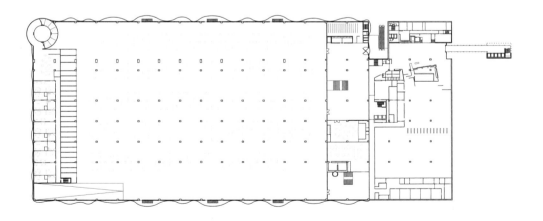

Laboratory EAST Modern Times Casino Herdern

Marc Bardelloni, Silouane Fellrath & Henri Wahlen

Scale 1:2500

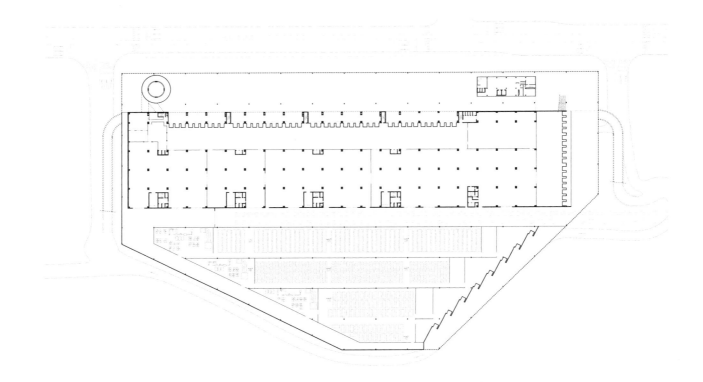

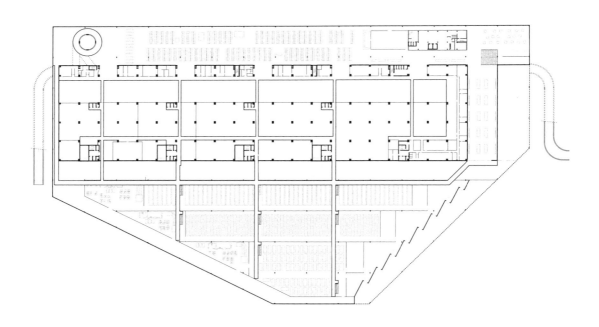

Scale 1:2500

Marie-Christine Béris & Robin Bollschweiler

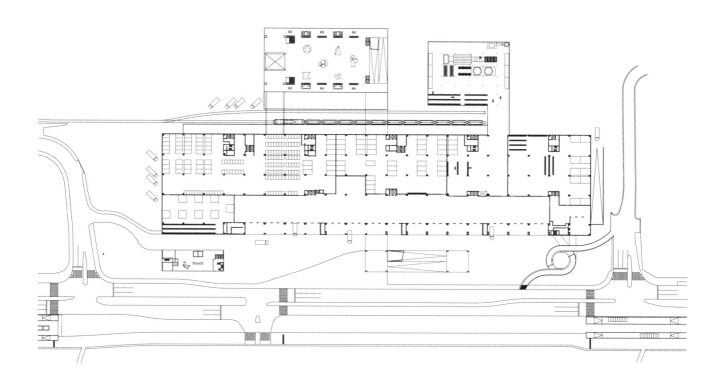

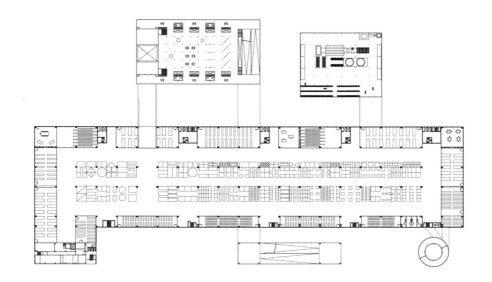

Ian Bichelmeier & Floriane Fol

Scale 1:2500

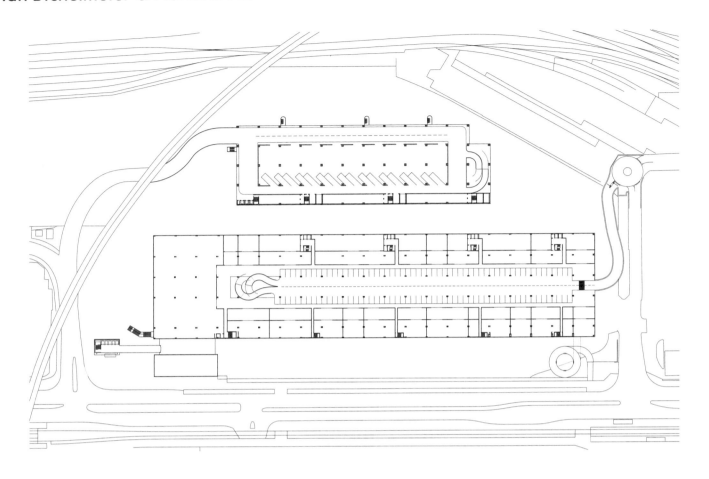

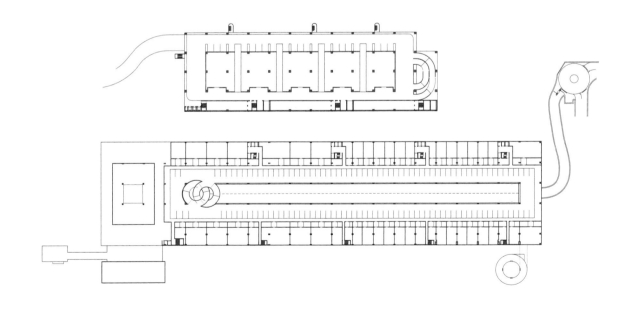

314   Mobility   Modern Times   Laboratory EAST

Scale 1:2500

Alicia Borchardt & Djuna Spagnoli

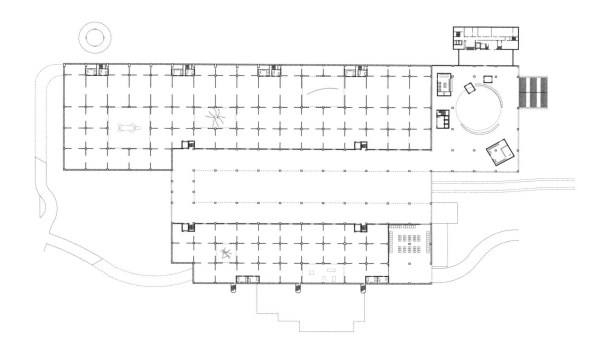

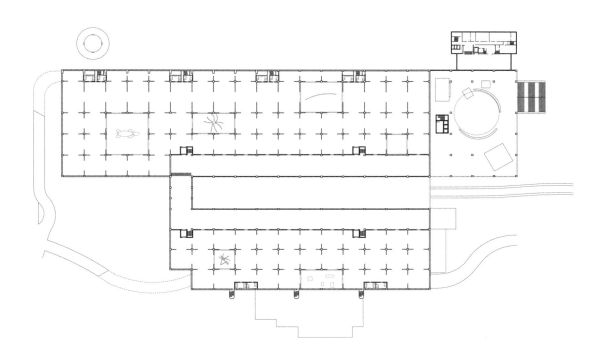

Laboratory EAST Modern Times Switch **317**

Emile Corthay & Jonas Inhelder

Scale 1:2500

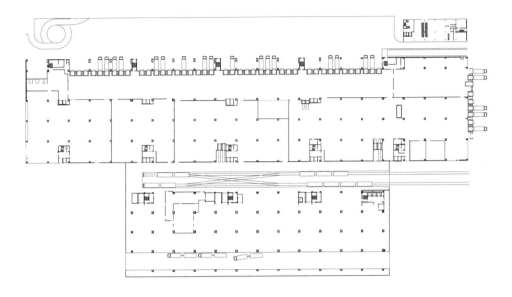

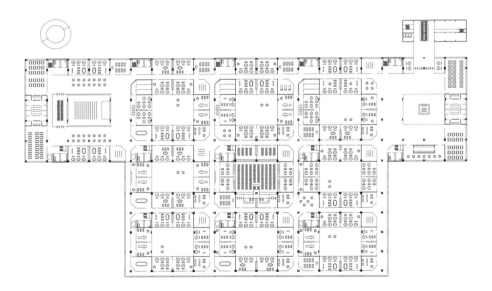

318   Data   Modern Times   Laboratory EAST

Scale 1:2500

Maya Déglon, Charlotte Din & Anne-Michèle Savoy

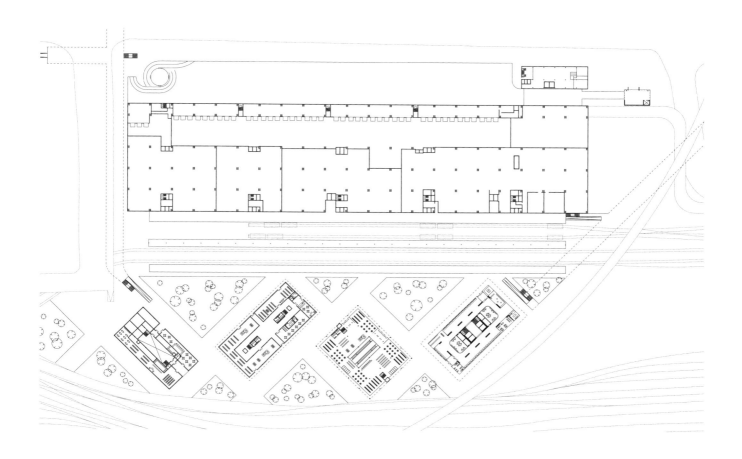

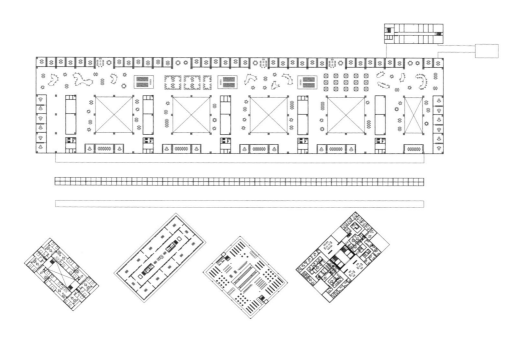

Laboratory EAST — Modern Times — M-City

Noemi Dolci & Fiona Uka

Scale 1:2500

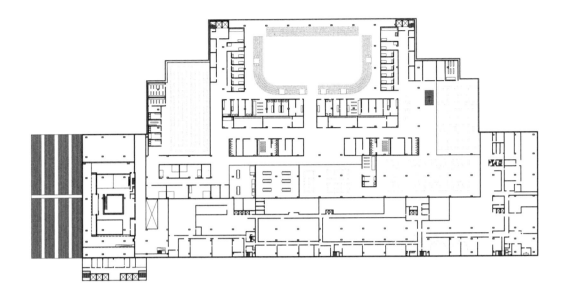

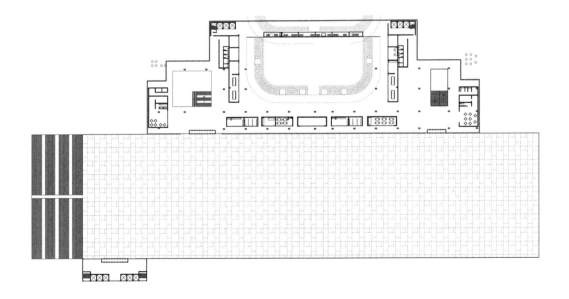

Scale 1:2500

Karoline Endres & Camille Paragon

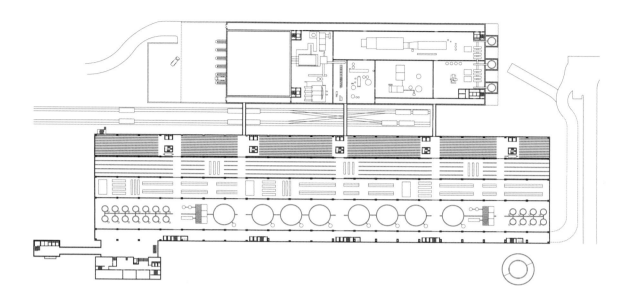

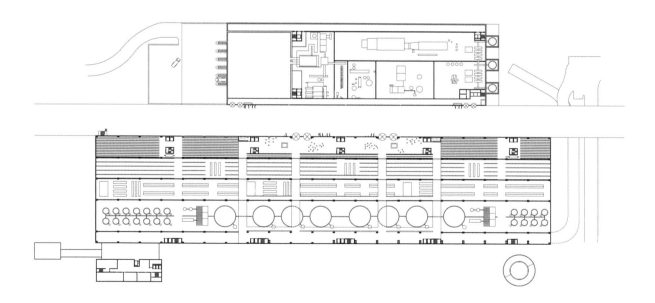

Laboratory EAST   Modern Times   Food Cycle   **325**

Michèle Fardel & Mélanie Lai

Scale 1:2500

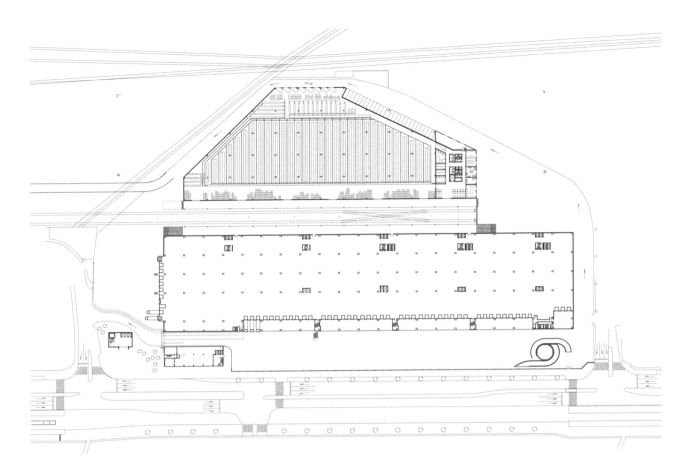

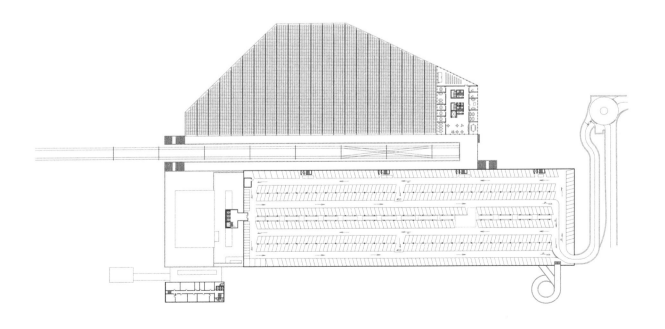

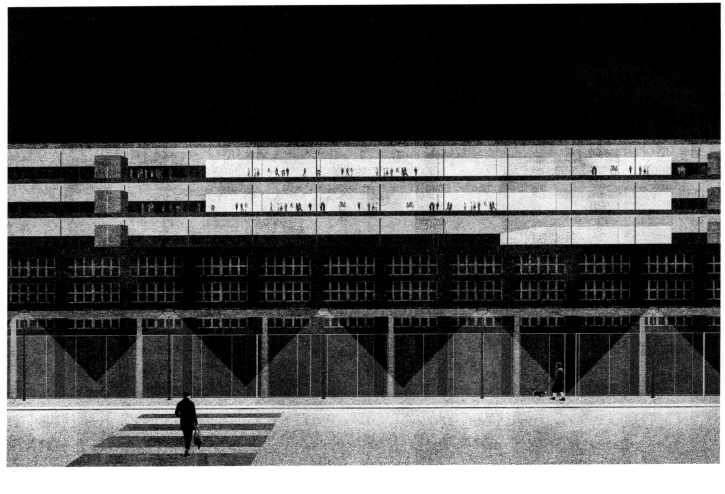

Scale 1:2500

Nila Goolaub & Pascal Rodrigues

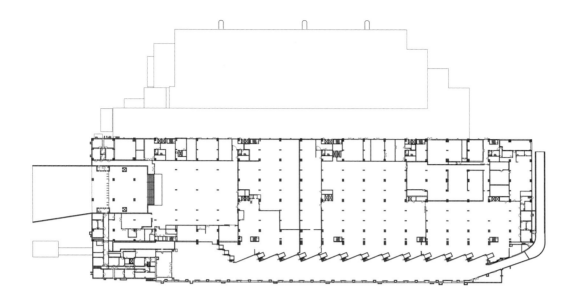

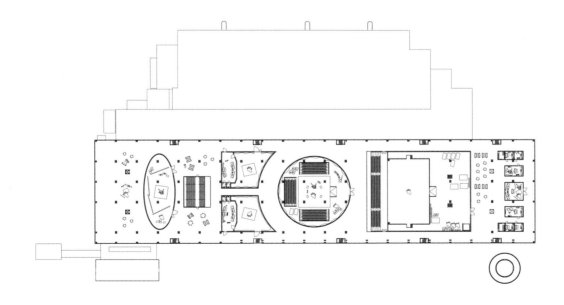

Laboratory EAST   Modern Times   When the levee breaks   **329**

Thomas Lutz & Matthieu Rapin

Scale 1:2500

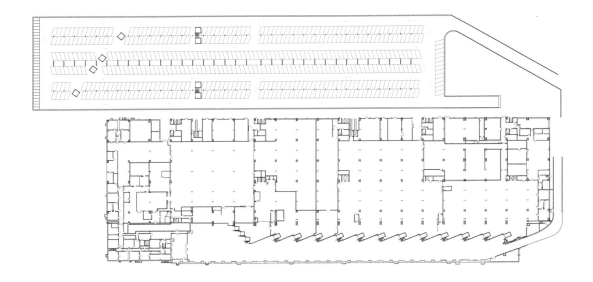

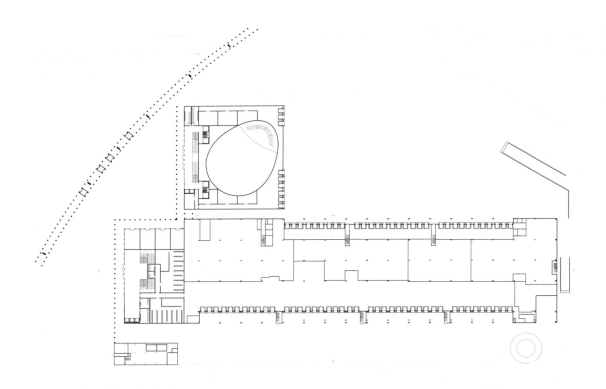

Scale 1:2500

Nina Mosca & Loris Thévenoz

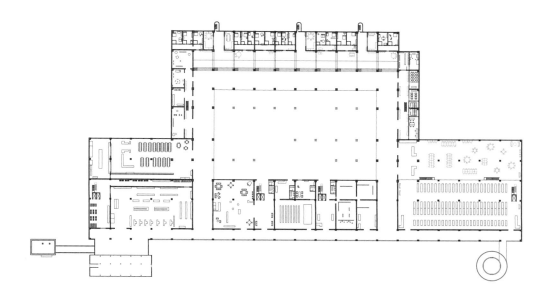

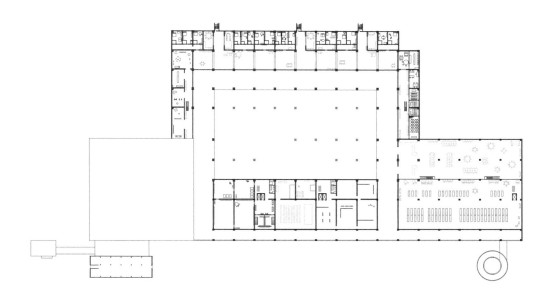

Laboratory EAST Modern Times Nostra Aetate

Sabine Uldry & Bénédicte Valla

Scale 1:2500

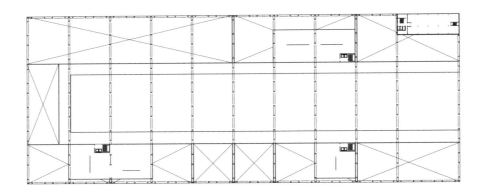

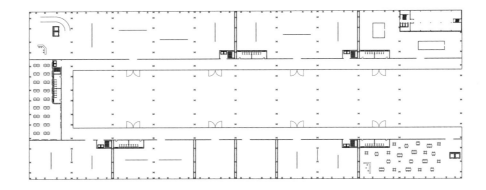

On Typology

Rafael Moneo

Part I

To raise the question of typology in architecture is to raise a question of the nature of the architectural work itself. To answer it means, for each generation, a redefinition of the essence of architecture and an explanation of all its attendant problems. This in turn requires the establishment of a theory, whose first question must be, what kind of object is a work of architecture? This question ultimately has to return to the concept of type.

On the one hand, a work of architecture has to be considered in its own right, as an entity in itself. That is, like other forms of art, it can be characterised by a condition of uniqueness. From this point of view, the work of architecture is irreducible within any classification. It is unrepeatable, a single phenomenon. Stylistic relationships may be recognised among architectural works, as in the other figurative arts, but they do not imply a loss of the singularity of the object.

On the other hand, a work of architecture can also be seen as belonging to a class of repeated objects, characterised, like a class of tools or instruments, by some general attributes. From the first hut to the archaic stone construction, primitive architecture conceived of itself as an activity similar to other kinds of craftsmanship, such as the making of textiles, pottery, baskets, and so on. The first products of this activity, which we in retrospect have called architecture, were no different from instruments or tools: building a primitive hut required solving problems of form and design similar in nature to those involved in weaving a basket, that is in making a useful object. Thus, like a basket or plate or cup, the architectural object could not only be repeated, but also was meant to be repeatable. Any changes that developed in it were particularities that could be found in any product of craftsmanship over time. In this sense, the uniqueness of the architectural object was denied. From this point of view a work of architecture, a construction, a house – like a boot, a cup, a helmet – can be defined through formal features, which express problems running from production to use, and which permit its reproduction. In these terms it can be said that the essence of the architectural object lies in repeatability.

The very act of naming the architectural object is also a process that from the nature of language is forced to typify. The identification of an architectural element like "column", or of a whole building – "courthouse" – implies an entire class of similar objects with common characteristics. This means that language also implicitly acknowledges the concept of type.

What then is type? It can most simply be defined as a concept which describes a group of objects characterised by the same formal structure. It is neither a spatial diagram nor the average of a serial list. It is fundamentally based on the possibility of grouping objects by certain inherent structural similarities. It might even be said that type means the act of thinking in groups. For instance, one may speak of skyscrapers in general; but the act of grouping pushes toward speaking of skyscrapers as huge, distorted Renaissance palaces, as Gothic towers, as fragmented pyramids, as oriented slabs…. Then, as one becomes increasingly precise, one introduces other levels of grouping, thus describing new ranks of types. One finishes with the name of a specific building.[1] Thus, the idea of type, which ostensibly rules out individuality, in the end has to return to its origins in the single work.

Architecture, however – the world of objects created by architecture – is not only described by types, it is also produced through them. If this notion can be accepted, it can be understood why and how the architect identifies his work with a precise type. He is initially trapped by the type because it is the way he knows. Later he can act on it; he can destroy it, transform it, respect it. But he starts from the type. The design process is a way of bringing the elements of a typology – the idea of a formal structure – into the precise state that characterises the single work.

But what accurately is a formal structure? One could attempt a series of opposing definitions. First the aspects of the Gestalt could be emphasised. This would mean speaking about centrality or linearity of clusters or grids, trying to characterise form in terms of a deeper geometry. In this sense, certain texts have described all covered centralised spaces, from the primitive hut to the Renaissance dome to that of the nineteenth century, as being of the same "type."[2] This however reduces the idea of type as formal structure to simple abstract geometry. But type as a formal structure is, in contrast, also intimately connected with reality – with a vast hierarchy of concerns running from social activity to building construction. Ultimately, the group defining a type must be rooted in this reality as well as in an abstract geometry. This means, for example, that buildings also have a precise position in history. In this sense nineteenth century domes belong to an entirely different rank of domes from those of the Renaissance or Baroque periods, and thereby constitute their own specific type.

This leads directly to the concept of a typological series that is generated by the relationship among the elements that define the whole. The type implies the presence of elements forming such a typological series and, of course, the elements can themselves be further examined and considered as single types; but their interaction defines a precise formal structure.

Thus, Brunelleschi introduced the lantern as a logical termination of the dome at Florence, and this form was imitated for almost three hundred years. The relationship between the Classical dome and post-Gothic lantern should be considered as one of the most characteristic features of Renaissance and post-Renaissance domes, giving them a certain formal consistency. When Enlightenment architects worked with domes they entirely changed the relationship between the elements that defined the formal structure – dome and lantern – thus generating a new type. Types are transformed, that is, one type becomes another, when substantial elements in the formal structure are changed.[3]

One of the frequent arguments against typology views it as a "frozen mechanism" that denies change and emphasises an almost automatic repetition.[4] However, the very concept of type, as it has been proposed here, implies the idea of change, or of transformation. The architect identifies the type on or with which he is working, but that does not necessarily imply mechanical reproduction. Of course, the typological approach *per se* does not demand constant change; and when a type is firmly consolidated, the resultant architectural forms preserve formal features in such a way as to allow works of architecture to be produced by a repetitive process, either an exact one as found in industry, or an approximate one as found in craftsmanship. But the consistency and stability of forms in such instances need not be attributed to the concept of type; it is just as possible to conclude that the struggle with an identical problem tends to lead to almost identical forms. Or in other words, stability in a society – stability reflected in activities, techniques, images – is mirrored also, in architecture.

The concept of type is in itself open to change insofar as it means a consciousness of actual facts, including, certainly, a recognition of the possibility of change. By looking at architectural objects as groups, as types, susceptible to differentiation in their secondary aspects, the partial obsolescence appearing in them can be appraised and consequently one can act to change them. The type can thus be thought of as the frame within which change operates, a necessary term to the continuing dialectic required by history. From this point of view, the type, rather than being a "frozen mechanism" to produce architecture, becomes a way of denying the past, as well as a way of looking at the future.

In this continuous process of transformation, the architect can extrapolate from the type, changing its use; he can distort the type by means of a transformation of scale; he can overlap different types to produce new ones. He can use formal quotations of a known type in a different context, as well as create new types by a radical change in the techniques already employed. The list of different mechanisms is extensive. It is a function of the inventiveness of architects.

The most intense moments in architectural development are those when a new type appears. One of the architect's greatest efforts, and thus the most deserving of admiration, is made when he gives up a known type and clearly sets out to formulate a new one. Often, external events — such as new techniques or changes in society — are responsible for impelling him toward this creation of a new type, in accordance with a dialectical relationship with history. But sometimes the invention of a new type is the result of an exceptional personality, capable of entering into architecture with its own voice.[5]

When a new type emerges — when an architect is able to describe a new set of formal relations which generates a new group of buildings or elements — then that architect's contribution has reached the level of generality and anonymity that characterises architecture as a discipline.

Part II

Given this close relation between type and the discipline of architecture, it is not surprising to find that the first coherent and explicit formulation of an idea of type in architectural theory was developed by Quatremère de Quincy at the end of the eighteenth century, precisely at the time when the traditional "discipline" of architecture had been thrown into question by emerging social and technical revolutions.[6]

For Quatremère the concept of type enabled architecture to reconstruct its links with the past, forming a kind of metaphorical connection with the moment when man, for the first time, confronted the problem of architecture and identified it in a form. In other words, the type explained the reason behind architecture, which remained constant throughout history, reinforcing through its continuity the permanence of the first moment in which the connection between the form and the nature of the object was understood and the concept of type was formulated. The type was thus intimately related with "needs and nature". "In spite of the industrious spirit which looks for innovation in objects", Quatremère writes, "who does not prefer the circular form to the polygonal for a human face? Who does not believe that the shape of a man's back must provide the type of the back of a chair? That the round shape must itself be the only reasonable type for the head's coiffure?"[7] The type was in this way identified with the logic of form connected with reason and use, and, throughout history, whenever an architectural object was related to some form, a kind of logic was implied, creating a deep bond with the past.

Based in this way on history, nature and use, the type had to be distinguished from the model — the mechanical reproduction of an object. Type expressed the permanence, in the single and unique object, of features which connected it with the past, acting as a perpetual recognition of a primitive but renewed identification of the condition of the object. Throughout the nineteenth century, however, the idea of type was applied in exactly the opposite way. Manuals and handbooks, so important for 19th century architectural knowledge, offered models or examples. The new importance assumed by programmes — a word that curiously does not appear in Quatremère's Dictionary — is in opposition to his concept of type-form and transfers the focus of theory to a new field, that of composition. Composition is the tool by which the architect deals with the variety of programmes offered by the new society; a theory of composition is needed to provide an instrument capable of coping with a diversity that, with difficulty, can be reduced to known types. Composition should be understood as the mechanism that resolves the connection between form and programme — or form and function — to which a new idea of architecture is wedded. It is from this point of view that the difference between Quatremère and someone like Durand can be seen.

For Durand, the first aim of the architecture is no longer the imitation of nature or the search for pleasure and artistic satisfaction, but composition or "disposition". This idea of composition is directly related to needs; its relevant criteria are, accordingly, convenience and economy. Convenience seeks solidity, salubrity and comfort; economy requires symmetry, regularity, and also simplicity — all attributes to be achieved with composition.

According to Durand, the architect disposes of elements — columns, pillars, foundations, vaults, and so on — which have taken form and proportion through their relationship with material and with use. These elements, argues Durand, must be freed from the tyranny of Orders; the Classical orders should be seen as mere decoration.[8] Having established the elements firmly through use and material, Durand says that the architect's task is to combine these elements, generating more complex entities, the parts of which will — at the end, through the composition — be assembled in a single building. Thus Durand offers a series of porches, vestibules, staircases, courts, etc. as parts of future buildings associated with precise programmes [Fig. 1 (frontispiece), 2–5]. These parts, ordered and presented like a repertoire of models, constitute the materials available to the architect. By using these parts, the architect can achieve architecture through composition and still retain responsibility for final unity — a Classical attribute that Durand does not deny to the building. But how to achieve this unity?

Durand proposes two instruments with which to handle the composition, to rule the construction of a building, whatever its programme: one is the continuous, undifferentiated grid; the other the use of the axis as a support for the reversal of its parts.

Both mechanisms are essentially contrary to Quatremère's idea of type as based on elemental and primitive forms. Quantification is now posed against qualification: on the grid and with the axis, programmes – buildings – could be flexible as well as desirable. The square grid ended the idea of architecture as it had been elaborated in the Renaissance and used until the end of the eighteenth century; the old definition of type, the original reason for form in architecture, was transformed by Durand into a method of composition based on a generic geometry of axes superimposed on the grid. The connection between type and form disappeared.

Durand himself avoided the idea of type; he used the word genre when, in the third part of his book, he described the variety of buildings classified according to their programmes. He collected, and sometimes even invented, hospitals, prisons, palaces, libraries, theatres, custom houses, barracks, town halls, colleges [Fig. 6]; a collection which presupposed a certain concern with type, although solely identified with the building's use. In so doing, he repeated the treatment he had adopted twenty years before in his *Recueil et parallèle des édifices de tout genre …*[9] in which temples, churches, squares and markets were categorised according to their programme or use – categories which interested him more than their forms and more than any related questions of style or language.

But in proposing a list of models, and afterward defining the rules and principles of composition, Durand's work anticipated the nineteenth century's theoretical approach to architecture: a knowledge based on history as a quarry of available material, supported by an idea of composition suggested by Durand's principles, elaborated and later finalised in the Beaux-Arts architectural system of the last years of the century. Durand would have understood, no doubt, why the battle of styles exploded with such virulence in the middle of the century. "Style" was something that could be added later, a final formal characterisation given to the elements after the structure of the building had been defined through a composition, which somehow reflected its programme.

Durand thereby offered a simple enough method of coping with the programmes and the new building requirements demanded by a new society. The demand that the object be repeatable was superseded by a new and different point of view whose basis was not sought in the nature of the architectural object. The conditions and attributes of the object itself which were central to Quatremère's inquiries ceased to be critical. It was the immediate responsibility of the architectural object as a theoretical instrument with an institutionalised role to make itself comprehensible as a product. Without doubt this new approach to architecture was related to the appearance of schools; as the product of the architect, architecture needed a body of doctrine – an idea of composition reinforced by a broader network of examples either of buildings or of single elements.

The handbooks and manuals which began to appear in the nineteenth century, following Durand's teachings, simply displayed the material available to the profession, classifying buildings by their function in a way that could be called typological. But however much well-defined single elements and vague and imprecise schematic plans for various kinds of programmes seemed to beget generic *partis* and thus seemed to suggest type forms, that total and indestructible formal structure which has been defined as type was irrevocably flattened. It had become a mere compositional and schematic device.

Part III

When, at the beginning of the twentieth century, a new sensibility sought the renovation of architecture, its first point of attack was the academic theory of architecture established in the nineteenth century. The theoreticians of the Modern Movement rejected the idea of type as it had been understood in the nineteenth century, for to them it meant immobility, a set of restrictions imposed on the creator who must, they posited, be able to act with complete freedom on the object. Thus when Gropius dispensed with history,[10] claiming that it was possible to undertake both the process of design and positive construction without reference to prior examples, he was standing against an architecture structured on typology. The nature of the architectural object thus changed once again. Architects now looked to the example of scientists in their attempt to describe the world in a new way. A new architecture must offer a new language, they believed, a new description of the physical space in which man lives. In this new field the concept of type was something quite alien and unessential.

This changed attitude toward the architect's product is clearly reflected in the work of Mies van der Rohe, in which the principles and aspirations of both Neoplasticism and the Bauhaus are joined, giving a certain degree of generality to the example. His work can be interpreted as an uninterrupted attempt to characterise a generic space, which could be called *the* space, of which architecture is simply the materialisation. According to this notion, the architect's task is to capture the idealised space through the definition of its abstract components. Like the physicist, the architect must first know the elements of matter, of space itself. He is then able to isolate a portion of that space to form a precise building. In constructing his building, he seizes this space and in doing so he constructs a building characterised not by its use – as a school, hospital, church, etc. in the manner of the nineteenth century – but a "space" in which an activity is produced only later. From this point of view, the I.I.T. campus must be understood more as a space – a physical fragment of a conceptual space – than as a set of buildings submitted to a process of architectural composition. The space is simply made available, it could be a church as well as a school. Mies was disturbed neither by functions nor materials; he was a builder of form-space.

Even when he designed a number of houses with the generic and quasi-typological designation of "courtyard houses" [Fig. 7], the designation was more an allusion to a well-known type than a reduplication of it. These houses are in the end defined by the way in which the architect has materialised space; the court itself does not structure their disposition: in them, space takes precedence over type. Thus the houses are understood as single aesthetic events in which the architect copes with a new reality. Whatever connection they have with the past – in architectonic terms, with the type – is carefully avoided in favour of a generic and actual description of the current world. For Modern Movement architects also wanted to offer a new image of architecture to the society that produced it, an image that reflected the new industrialised world created by that society. This meant that a mass-production system had to be introduced into architecture, thus displacing the quality of singularity and uniqueness of the traditional architectural "object". The type as the artificial species described by Quatremère and the type as the "average" of models proclaimed by the theoreticians of the nineteenth century now had to be put aside; the industrial processes had established a new relationship between production and object which was far removed from the experience of any precedents. Taken to its logical conclusion, such an attitude toward mass production was in clear contradiction to the Modern Movement's own preoccupation with the unique spatial object. But with regard to the idea of type, both aspects of Modern Movement theory, however contradictory, coincided in their rejection of type as a key to understanding the architectural object.

Mass production in architecture, focused chiefly on mass housing, permitted architecture to be seen in a new light. Repeatability was desirable, as it was consonant with industry. "The same constructions for the same requirements", Bruno Taut wrote,[11] and now the word "same" needed to be understood *ad litteram*. Industry required repetition, series; the new architecture could be pre-cast. Now the word type – in its primary and original sense of permitting the exact reproduction of a model – was transformed from an abstraction to a reality in architecture, by virtue of industry; type had become prototype.

This could be seen in Le Corbusier's work where the contradiction between architecture as a single and unique event and architecture as a process of elaboration of industrial prototypes is clearly marked. From the beginning, Le Corbusier was interested in this condition of an industrial prototype allowing for limitless repetition. The Domino house, of all the "industrialised" schemes proposed by Le Corbusier in the Twenties and early Thirties, insists on this theme as do the towers in the Plan Voisin or in the Ville Radieuse [Fig. 8]. Later, the Unite d'Habitation becomes a clear example of such an attitude: it can be readapted – Marseilles, Nantes, Berlin – without alteration; it is a unit, the result of factory production processes, capable of being sent anywhere. In Le Corbusier's theory, the building industry should be analogous to the auto industry; like primitive architecture, but now through the industrial process, the new architecture should return to its former status as a typal instrument.

This new idea of type effectively denied the concept of type as it had been conceived in the past. The singularity of the architectural object which in the nineteenth century had permitted adaptability to site and flexibility for use within the framework of a structure was violently denied by the new architecture, committed to architecture as mass production.

But there was a third argument against the nineteenth century's concept of typology. This argument was provided by functionalism. Functionalism – the cause/effect relationship between requirements and form – seemed to provide the rules for architecture without recourse to precedents, without need for the historical concept of type. And, although functionalist theory was not necessarily coincident with the other two attitudes already described, all three had in common the rejection of the past as a form of knowledge in architecture. Yet each followed a different path; functionalism was mainly concerned with method, while the other two dealt with figurative space and production respectively. The unique qualities of each problem, of each precise context for which functionalism seemed to provide a unique resolution, seemed to be posed against the idea of a common structure that characterised type. Architecture was predetermined not by types, but by context itself. As an almost inevitable conclusion, architectural theories connected with functionalism deliberately rejected typology.

Paradoxically, functionalist theory, which explicitly stood against typology, also provided the basis for a new understanding of the idea of type. This consciousness of type appears in the work of architects such as Taut, May, Stam, etc., who were grouped around the CIAM congress, and can be found in a number of writings – for example the classic work by F.R.S. Yorke on *The Modern Flat*.[12]

The attitude perhaps becomes most explicit in the work of Alexander Klein. Klein's attempt to systematise all the elements of the single house in his *Das Einfamilienhaus* was a clear and new approach to the problem [Figs. 9, 10].[13] While recognising the value of the type as a structure underlying and giving form to the elements of any architecture, he was at the same time able to modify and explore the type without accepting it as the inevitable product of the past. In so doing, he attempted to submit the elements – identified now in terms of use – to the rationality of typology by checking dimensions, clarifying circulation, emphasising orientation. The type seemed to lose both the abstract and obscure characterisation of Quatremère and the frozen description of the academics. Housing types appeared flexible, able to be adapted to the exigencies of both site and programme. For Klein, the types, far from being an imposition of history, became a working instrument. Their starting point was the site of the Modern Movement's failure: the traditional city.

Part IV

Against the failure of the Modern Movement to use type in terms of the city, a new series of writings began to appear in the Sixties which called for a theory to explain the formal and structural continuity of traditional cities. These saw the city as a formal structure which could be understood through its continuous historical development. From this point of view architecture was considered neither as the single artistic event proposed by the avant garde nor the industrially produced object, but now as a process, in time, of building from the single dwelling to the total city. Accordingly, in Saverio Muratori's *Studi per una operante Storia Urbana di Venezia*, the urban texture of Venice was examined, and the idea of type as formal structure became a central idea that demonstrated a continuity among the different scales of the city. For Muratori, type was not so much an abstract concept as an element that allowed him to understand the pattern of growth of the city[14] as a living organism taking its meaning primarily from its history. He explained the historical development of Venice as a concept that would link the individual elements with the overall form of the city. These types were seen as the generators of the city and implicit in them were the elements that defined all other scales; so, for example, in Venice *calli*, *campi* and *corti* are seen as typal elements which are intimately related with each other, and each is without meaning if not considered as types in themselves.

This approach, underlining the relationship between the elements and the whole, proposed a morphological method of analysis for understanding architecture, which has formed the basis for a continued development of typological studies. In the second half of the Sixties, it finds its most systematic and complex theoretical development in the work of Aldo Rossi and his circle. But this emphasis on morphology, reducing typology exclusively to the field of urban analysis, was complemented by a renewed interest in the concept of type as first postulated by Quatremère and renewed by "Typologia" by G.C. Argan.[15]

Argan returned to the origins of the concept, interpreting Quatremère's definition in a more pragmatic way and avoiding the Neoplatonism that it implied. For Argan the type was a kind of abstraction inherent in the use and form of series of buildings. Its identification, however, in as much as it was deduced from reality, was inescapably an *a posteriori* operation. Here Argan differed radically from Quatremère, whose idea of type approached that of a Platonic absolute – an *a priori* "form". For Argan it was through the comparison and overlapping of certain formal regularities that the type emerged; it was the basic form through which series of buildings were related to each other in a comprehensible way. Type, in this sense, could be defined as the "inner formal structure" of a building or series of buildings. But if the type was part of such an overall structure, how could it be connected with the individual work? The notion of type propounded by Quatremère as "something vague, undefined" provided this answer. The architect could work on types freely because there were two moments, "the moment of the typology and the moment of the formal definition", which could be distinguished from one another. For Argan, "the moment of typology" was the non-problematic moment, implying a certain degree of inertia. This moment, which established a necessary connection with the past and with society, was in some way a "natural" given, received and not invented by the form-defining artist. However, Argan gave primacy to the second, the form-defining moment – that is, he did not see typology, although inevitable, as the primary characteristic of architecture. In this way he revealed his respect for Modem Movement orthodoxy. And yet, the very concept of type, as has been seen, opposed both Modern Movement ideology and the studies in design method which became its natural extension in the Sixties.

If, as argued by the methodologists, architecture was the formal expression of its various requirements, and if the links between such requirements and reality could be defined, then architecture as a problem of method could be entirely resolved. Form, however, is in reality a product of an entirely opposite methodology – and not the result of method as was previously understood. In this sense, Ernesto Rogers, following Argan, was able to oppose the concept of type-form to the concept of methodology.[16] Knowledge in architecture, he proposed, implied the immediate acceptance of "types". Types were part of a framework defined by reality which characterised and classified all single events. Within this framework, the architect worked; his work was a continuous comment on the past, on the prior knowledge on which his work was based. According to Ernesto Rogers's theory the design process started with the architect's identification of a type which would resolve the problem implicit in the context within which he was working.

Of course, the identification of such a type was a choice by virtue of which the architect inevitably established ties with society. By transforming the necessarily "vague, undefined" type in a single act, his work acquired a certain consistency with a specific context. From this point of view, his work could be seen as a contribution to the contextualisation of a more genetic type. Thus, the development of a project was a process that led from the abstract type to the precise reality. In other words, through the concept of type, the architect was provided with an instrument that allowed him to undertake the design process in quite a different way than that demanded by the methodological approach. Rogers's theory in this way resembled a more traditional approach. It was Aldo Rossi who in the late Sixties bound together the morphological approach of Muratori and the more traditional approach of Rogers and Argan through Quatremère. In so doing he introduced a more subtle but also problematic notion of type.

For Rossi the logic of architectural form lies in a definition of type based on the juxtaposition of memory and reason.[17] Insofar as architecture retains the memory of those first moments in which man asserted and established his presence in the world through building activity, so type retains the reason of form itself. The type preserves and defines the internal logic of forms, not by techniques or programmes – in fact, the type can be called "functionally indifferent". In Rossi's idea of architecture, the corridor, for example, is a primary type; it is indifferently available to the programme of an individual house and to a student residence or a school.

Because the city, or its builders, has lost its own memory and forgotten the value of these primary and permanent types, according to Rossi, the task of architects today is to contribute to their recovery. Thus the city Rossi, the silent witness, pictures is one in which time seems to be frozen. If it is unrecognisable as any specific place, this is because for him there is only one ideal city, filled with types (rather impure types, but types nonetheless), and the history of architecture is none other than its history.

Within the city are contained the principles of the architectural discipline, and the proof of their autonomy is given by the permanence of types through history. Yet the very silence and autonomy of Rossi's images of these types within the ideal city that encloses them graphically raise the question of their relation to reality – to a real society – and thereby the question of their actualisation and contextualisation. Rossi's types communicate only with themselves and their ideal context. They become only mute reminders of a more or less perfect past, a past that may not even have existed.

But another critic, Alan Colquhoun, has suggested that the possibility of a real communication between architecture and society is not necessarily precluded by the idea of type.[18] Indeed, a certain level of reality – which is necessary if communication is desired – is centrally concerned with types, because it is through the concept of type that the process of communication is made possible. Thus, denying the possibility of an architecture unrelated to intelligible forms of the past – that is unrelated to types – Colquhoun understands architecture as a discipline of conventions; but precisely because of its conventionality, it is arbitrary and therefore susceptible to voluntary changes. In other words, the architect masters meaning and, through it, he is able to enter into the process of society's transformation.

Colquhoun's definition of type as a support of intelligibility presents another possibility from which typology can be observed, and in a sense rediscovered: that is, as an explanation of architecture from an ideological point of view. This would allow for the establishment of links between architecture and society.[19] Within this other view, the architect has, whether he likes it or not, the obligation and the duty to deal with ideological content. The types – the materials with which the architect works – are seen to be coloured by ideology and assume meaning within the structural framework in which architecture is produced. In accepting a type, or in rejecting it, the architect is thus entering into the realm of communication in which the life of the individual man is involved with that of society. The architect thus makes his "voluntary decisions" in the world of types, and these "voluntary decisions" explain the ideological position of the architect. As he works with types, his thought and his position are incorporated into them. If a work of architecture needs the type to establish a path for its communication – to avoid the gap between the past, the moment of creation, and the world in which the architecture is ultimately placed – then types must be the starting point of the design process.

Such an attitude toward typology proposes a new level of meaning for architectural objects in history, one that relates to their place in the public realm and their integral position in society, not as autonomous objects but as elements given life by the process of history itself. Thus, in the words of George Kubler "the time of history is too coarse and brief to be an evenly granular duration such as the physicists suppose for natural time; it is more like a sea occupied by innumerable forms of a finite number of types."[20] The history of art, and therefore the history of architecture, would be the description of the "life" of these types.

Part V

But despite this rediscovery of the concept of type in recent years, it is perhaps not so easy to find it accepted as an active fact in contemporary architecture. We are continually being presented with ideas and images of type which seem to be in complete disjunction with their supposed realisation. Thus while Louis Kahn's search[21] for origins as a primary condition of architecture allowed us to think in terms of a possible rebirth of Quatremère's ideas, this attitude was not necessarily present in the work of his followers. They merely imitated the language of this attempted return to origins without respecting the search itself. While it is also true that the impact of the structuralist approach on the type concept has been pervasively present in a large number of projects connected with the recent Neo-rationalist movement, most of these projects confirm the existence of a new typological attitude dialectically opposed to the context in which they act.[22] However these projects present an important question. Can the same definition of type which enabled these architects to explain the growth and continuity of the traditional city in terms of its formal structure be used to propose new "types" in contradiction to this structure? That is, can such new projects be considered as strictly typological if they merely explain the growth of the old cities? In the works of the Krier brothers the new vision of the city certainly incorporates the structural component implicit in the typological approach to the old city; the city that they draw is a complex space in which the relationship and continuity between the different scales of elements is the most characteristic feature [Figs. 11]. But they are in reality providing only a "typological view" of this city: they are not building the city itself by using the concept of type. Thus, the relationship between city and place, city and time, that was earlier resolved by types has been broken. The city that grows by the successive addition of single elements, each with its own integrity, has been lost forever. The only alternative now seems to be the reproduction of the old city. The concept of type that was observed in the old city is used to structure the new forms, providing them with formal consistency, but no more than that. In other words, typology today has come to be understood simply as a mechanism of composition. The so-called "typological" research today merely results in the production of images, or in the reconstitution of traditional typologies. In the end it can be said that it is the nostalgia for types that gives formal consistency to these works.

The "impossibility" of continuity, and thus of the retrieval of type in its most traditional and characteristic sense, is underlined by the renewed emphasis on communication – on meaning and signification in architecture. An example of this can be found in the work of Robert Venturi. For example, in his houses in Nantucket the typical image of the wooden American house is clearly sought [Figs. 12, 13]. Nevertheless, while Venturi seems to have tried to maintain the image of the vernacular house on the outside, the inner structure lacks any resemblance to or memory of the old. Only the outer image remains, and into this image Venturi introduces as many elements as he needs – windows, staircases, etc. – without much concern for his original model. Thus, these houses defined by image contain a great variety of elements characterised only by their generality, and while these elements are almost standard, they are lacking in any kind of explicit relationship with the formal structure. The architect handles them as known materials, entities in themselves, without feeling the necessity to establish any linkage to a continuous formal structure. Moreover, in spite of the generality of the elements, the houses are very precise and singular events and can be considered neither the expression of a known type nor a potentially bold appearance of a new prototype.

For Venturi, type is reduced to image, or better, the image is the type, in the belief that through images communication is achieved. As such, the type-image is more concerned with recognition than with structure.

The result is an architecture in which a unifying image is recognised whose elements belong clearly to architectural history, but in which the classic interdependence of the elements is definitively lost. The type as inner formal structure has disappeared, and as single architectural elements take on the value of type-images, each becomes available to be considered in its singleness as an independent fragment.

Here, in fact, one is confronted with a broken structure, shattered into formally autonomous pieces. Venturi has intentionally broken the idea of a typological unity which for centuries dominated architecture. He finds, however, and not without shock, that the image of architecture emerges again in the broken mirror. Architecture, which in the past has been an imitative art, a description of nature, now seems to be so again, but this time with architecture itself as a model. Architecture is indeed an imitative art, but now imitative of itself, reflecting a fragmented and discontinuous reality.

The architecture of Rossi initially seems to stand against this discontinuity. For here the unifying formal structure of type disappears. In spite of Rossi's strenuous defence of the concept of type in the construction stage of his work, a subtle formal dissociation occurs and the unity of the formal structure is broken. This dissociation is exemplified in Rossi's house, where the almost wall-like structure of the plan is connected with the *pilotis* below and the vaulted roof above. There is an almost deliberate provocation in this breakdown and recombination of types. In a highly sophisticated manner, Rossi reminds us of our knowledge – and also our ignorance – of types; they appear broken but bearing unexpected power. It might be said that a nostalgia for an impossible orthodoxy emerges out of this architecture. In the work of Rossi, and even that of Venturi, a discomforting thought arises: was it not perhaps at the very point when the idea of type became clearly articulated in architectural theory – at the end of the eighteenth century – that the reality of its existence, its traditional operation in history, became finally impossible?

Did not the historical awareness of the fact of type in architectural theory forever bar the unity of its practice? Or to put it in a different way, is not the theoretical recognition of a fact the symptom of its loss? Hence the extreme difficulty of applying the concept of type to current architecture, in spite of our awareness of its value in explaining a historical tradition.

Changes in techniques and society – and therefore in the relationship between an institutionalised profession and its architectural product – have led to a deep transformation in the old theoretical patterns. The continuity in structure, activities and form which in the past allowed for the consistent use of types has been seriously broken in modern times. Beyond this, the general lack of faith which characterises the present world in any collective and widely shared opinion naturally does not support the fixing of types.

It seems that type can no longer define the confrontation of internal ideology and external constraints. Since formal structure must now support itself without the help of external circumstances (techniques, uses …), it is hardly surprising that architecture has taken heed of itself and looked for self-protection in the variety of images offered by its history. As Hannah Arendt has written recently, "something very similar seems at first glance to be true of the modern scientist who constantly destroys authentic semblances without, however, destroying his own sensation of reality, which tells him, as it tells us, that the sun rises in the morning and sets in the evening."[23]

The only sensation of reality left for architecture today resides in its history. The world of images provided by history is the only sensible reality that has not been destroyed by scientific knowledge or by society. The broken types are the "authentic semblances" of this reality, broken through the long process that has been described briefly in these pages. Fragmentation seems to be in these days the concomitant of type; it is, in the end, the only remaining weapon left to the architect after having given over to the architectural object its own single identity, while forgetting, very often, the specificity of the work of architecture.

The object – first the city, then the building itself – once broken and fragmented, seems to maintain its ties with the traditional discipline only in images of an ever-more distant memory. Thus, the culmination of the process beginning in a classic, post-Renaissance condition of form-type is its total destruction. The traditional typological approach, which has tried to recover the old idea of architecture, has largely failed. Thus, perhaps the only means architects have to master form today is to destroy it.

Ultimately, the question which remains is, does it make sense to speak of type today? Perhaps the impossibility of directly applying old definitions to new situations has been demonstrated, but this does not mean, however, that the interest and value of the concept of type is thereby denied completely. To understand the question of type is to understand the nature of the architectural object today. It is a question that cannot be avoided. The architectural object can no longer be considered as a single, isolated event because it is bounded by the world that surrounds it as well as by its history. It extends its life to other objects by virtue of its specific architectural condition, thereby establishing a chain of related events in which it is possible to find common formal structures. If architectural objects allow us to speak about both their singleness and their shared features, then the concept of type is of value, although the old definitions must be modified to accommodate an idea of type that can incorporate even the present state, where, in fact, subtle mechanisms of relationship are observable and suggest typological explanations.

1   See the way in which sky-scrapers have been grouped: W. Weisman in his article "A New View of Skyscraper History", *The Rise of an American Architecture*, Edgar Kaufmann, Jr., ed. (New York: The Metropolitan Museum of Art, 1970).

2   Such an approach can be found in the work of C. Norberg-Schulz, *Intentions in Architecture* (Cambridge, MA., 1963) and *Existence, Space, Architecture* (London, 1971). For him "centralization is the factor common to all domes".

3   There are no substantial differences between Renaissance and nineteenth-century domes. They must be considered as single types because of their relatively similar image.

4   See Bruno Zevi's arguments in *Architettura in Nuce* (Venice, 1960), p. 169.

5   Brunelleschi's intervention in Santa Maria del Fiore, Florence, is an evident example.

6   Quatremère de Quincy, *Dictionnaire Historique de l'Architecture* (Paris, 1832), pp. 629–30. A complete study of Quatremère's definition and its relationship with the social and ideological background can be found in Anthony Vidler's article in *Oppositions*, 8 (Spring 1977).

7   Ibid., p. 630.

8   J. N. L. Durand, *Précis des Lesons d'Architecture*, XIII (Paris, 1805).

9   J. N. L. Durand, *Recueil et Parallele des Edifices de Tout Genre, Anciens et Modernes*, IX (Paris, 1801).

10 See Walter Gropius, *Scope of total Architecture* (New York, 1955).

11 Bruno Taut, *Modern Architecture* (London, 1929).

12 F.R.S. Yorke, *The Modern House* (London, 1934); *The Modern Flat* (London 1934).

13 Alexander Klein, *Das Einfamilienhaus* (Stuttgart, 1934). The renewed interest in current years by the typological problem has been responsible for a certain rediscovery of Klein's works. A clear example of this trend would be the book by G. Grassi, *La costruzione logica dell'architettura* (Padua, 1967).

14 Saverio Muratoni, *Studi per una operante storia urbana di Venezia* (Rome, 1960). See also Massimo Scolari, "Un contributo per la fondazione della scienza urbana," *Controspazio*, no. 7–8 (1971). [Abridged and edited footnote]

15 The already classic "Quatremère quotation" comes from G.C. Argan, who introduced the subject in his article on "Tipologia" in the *Enciclopedia Universale dell' Arte* published by the Istituto per la Collaborazione Culturale, Venice. Later the text was reprinted in the book *Progetto e Destino* (Milan, 1965).

16 See E. Rogers, "Esperienza di un Corso Universitario", *La Utopia della Realta* (Bari, 1965). See also Oriol Bohigas's article "Metodologia y Tipologia", *Contra una Arquitectura adjetivada* (Barcelona, 1969), which follow Rogers's paths.

17 There exists a large body of writing on Rossi's work and his idea of type. One complete book with a key to both the writings and the criticism about it is Rossi's *Scritti, scelti sull'architettura e la citta*, ed. Rosaldo Bonicalzi (Milan, 1975) … See also E. Bonfanti, "Elementi e Costruzione. Note sull'architettura di Aldo Rossi," Controspazio, no. 10 (1970); and M. Scolari, "Un contributo per la fondazione della scienza urbana,", Vittorio Savi, *L'architettura di Aldo Rossi* (Milan, 1976), Moreover, it is also important in studying Rossi to pay attention to the work of people close to him, like Carlo Aymonino – see, for instance, Aymonino's contlibutions to *Considerazioni sulla morfologia urbana e la tipologia edilizia* (Venice, 1964); *Rapporti tra mofologia urbana e tipologia edilizia* (Venice, 1966); La formazione del concetto di tipologia edilizia* (Venice, 1965); *La citta di Padova* (Rome, 1970). On Giorgio Grassi, see L. Semerani, G. U. Polessello, et al., *La Costruzione logica dell'architettura* (Padua, 1967). See also Massimo Scolari's article "Avanguardia e Nuova Architettura", *Architettura Razionale* (Milan, 1973). [Abridged and edited footnote]

18 Alan Colquhoun, "Typology and Design Method", *Arena, Journal of the Architectural Association*, June (1967); republished in Charles Jencks and George Baird, *Meaning in Architecture* (London, 1969).

19 It is not surprising that an architect as preoccupied with communication as Robert Venturi has paid special attention to Colquhoun's article. Cf. *Learning from Las Vegas* (Cambridge, MA, 1972).

20 George Kubler, *The Shape of Time* (New Haven, 1962), p. 32.

21 Cf. his lecture, "Form and Design", *Architectural Design* (April 1961).

22 Often the typological analysis is used primarily as a term of reference to underscore the virtue of the proposed design.

23 Hannah Arendt, "Reflections: Thinking", *New Yorker*, 21, 28 November 1977 and *New Yorker*, 5 December, 1977.

This text was originally published in *Oppositions, Journal for Ideas and Criticism in Architecture*, 13. (Cambridge, MA: Institute for Architecture and Urban Studies, MIT Press, Summer 1978). The format of the footnote apparatus has been amended to match the current publication. The images accompanying the original essay have likewise been cut to match, but the captions are those in the original.

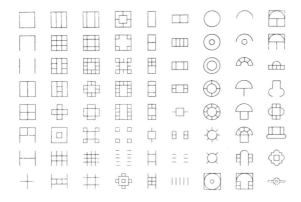

[Fig. 1]
J. N. L. Durand, Building forms, 1809. Frontispiece

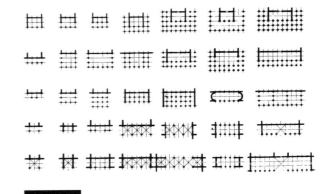

[Fig. 3]
J. N. L. Durand, Plan for porches, 1809.

[Fig. 2]
J. N. L. Durand, Façade combinations, 1809.

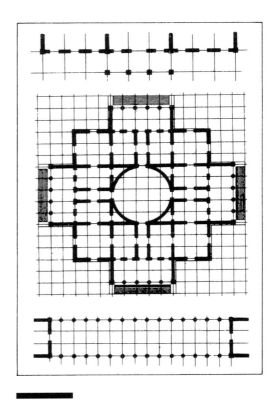

[Fig. 4]
J. N. L. Durand, Plan combinations, 1809.

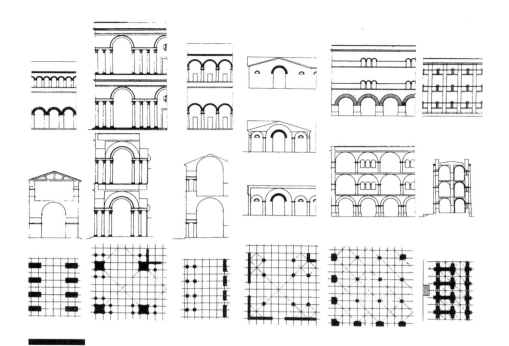

[Fig. 5]
J. N. L. Durand, Façade combinations, 1809.

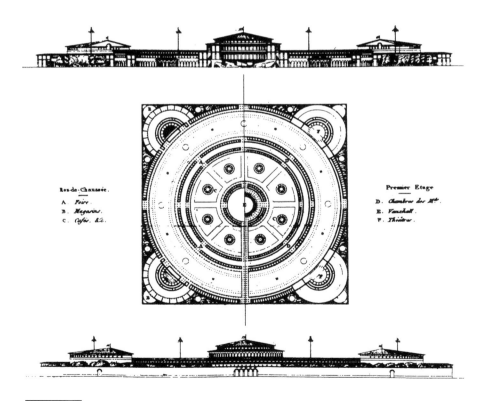

[Fig. 6]
J. N. L. Durand, Prototype for a fairground, 1809.

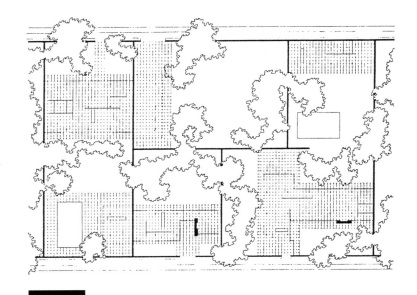

[Fig. 7]
Mies van der Rohe, Courtyard houses, 1938. Plan.

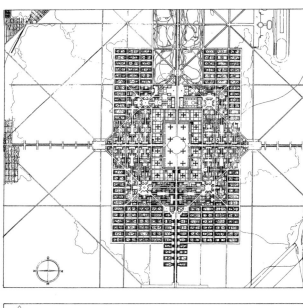

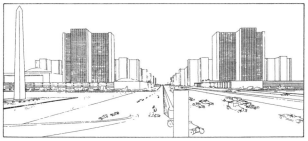

[Fig. 8]
Le Corbusier, La Ville Contemporaine, 1922. Project.

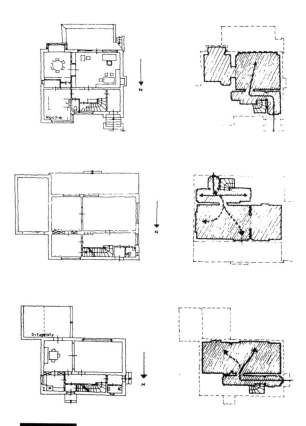

[Fig. 9]
Alexander Klein, Single-family house plans and circulation diagrams, 1934.

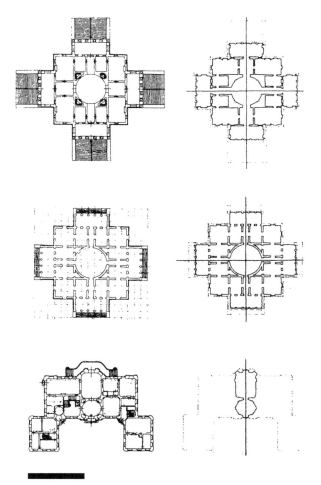

[Fig. 10]
Alexander Klein, Analysis of building plans, 1934.

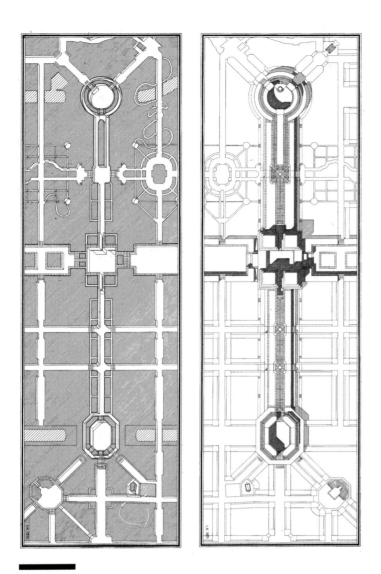

[Fig. 11]
Leon Krier, Leinfelden project, 1971.

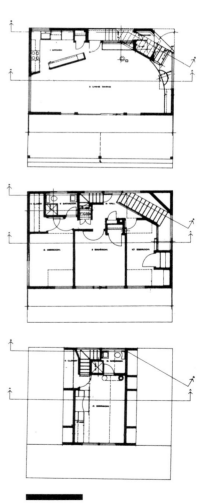

[Fig. 12]
Venturi and Rauch, Trubeck house, 1970. Plans.

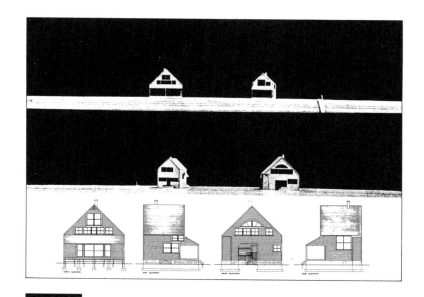

[Fig. 13]
Venturi and Rauch, Trubeck and Wislocki houses, Massachusetts, 1970. Elevations.

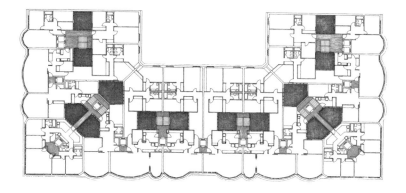

[Fig. 14]
Rafael Moneo with Javier Marquet, Javier Unzurunzaga and Luis M. Zulaica, Urumea Residential Building, San Sebastian, 1968–73. Typical plan.

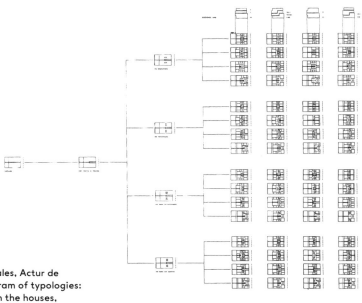

[Fig. 15]
Rafael Moneo with Manuel de Solà-Morales, Actur de Lacua. competition, Vitoria, 1977. Diagram of typologies: changes in the stairs allow for variety in the houses, producing the present tree.

Tackle the Type

An interview with Rafael Moneo on typology

Tiago P. Borges & Martin Fröhlich
Madrid, 15 November 2018

Forty years after your seminal text, is it still possible to talk about typological studies as a relevant working tool, and if so, in what sense?
The first thing to say when talking about typology as a tool is that not all architectural operations should be thought of in the same way. As a concept, you'll find that "type" can be applied directly more often than you'd think, in designs, commissions or projects. Nevertheless, I believe type is a concept that embraces a lot of architectural operations. It's not that easy to escape it; but that doesn't mean that everything you do should be subsumed in the notion of type. There are designs where the concept of "knowledge" is ... I'm not saying that this is enough, but it could be able to solve the designs that come out from new practices. The alternative is another kind of spirit has to flow into the design, and where, therefore, I still believe the notion of type lies behind a lot of architectural work. To identify this idea, one needs to be quite open. When I consider type, I also need to consider knowledge, and I try to establish some kind of association on the drawing table of an architect ... if the drawing table is still alive. If you look at the notion of type in architectural terms, you know it came directly out of the attempt to figure out how the form of cities should be understood. Today it's quite difficult to accept that the notion of morphology – related to the notion of type – can be applied in the same terms we use when talking about old traditional cities. It was a relevant perspective to understand how cities grew until the last century: though, it would be difficult to say that cities are growing today like they did years ago, so one needs to apply the notion of morphology and type in other terms. I believe it is a difficult notion to be used today.

**What is interesting about your essay is that you start from the notion that the idea of type belongs to the essence of architecture. Aldo Rossi also explored this approach, but we have the feeling that your article painted a more pessimistic perspective. In the end, you seem to suggest there are only fragments of that notion left – and this can maybe also be applied to a city made out of fragments – and that you questioned if it still made sense to speak about types in today's world.
Listening to you now, you seem to be less pessimistic and more open, and you sound as if you're suggesting that it makes less sense to talk about types. Would that be correct?**
I still sustain things the way I started the article forty years ago. No doubts. When you consider that buildings can be thought of as a sole entity, then a building has some formal structure in itself that allows you

to establish all the readings you want to have from it: in construction terms, in programmatic terms, in figurative or iconographic terms – all of them matter. But today you could say that the notion of buildings has been softened, or has lost a bit of the energy it used to have. When you talk about the very strong formal presence of a building today, the notion you are applying is that of iconography. The thinking is that the identity of a building is much more linked to the way it presents itself in the universe of built works, giving it an autonomous entity, not only in the context of cities. The belief still is that fragmented collections of buildings make a city; but cities always impose a certain sense of relationship between one building and others. I would say that when the notion of types was reassumed in the 1960s, the late 1950s, the thing was to try to give an answer to this mutual relationship between buildings and cities.

This connection between type and morphology ... the people who like to use the type, they like to look at the city as its larger and more extended reality, as something that is able to embrace everything that has been built. What I mean is that we can use the notion of type without thinking of buildings as establishing a certain continuity with others. I think of the Palladian villa as a type of construction that doesn't ask for morphology, but simply for a more generic viewpoint. At this moment where we are, buildings are thought of as objects. I would say that in general architectural criticism has used the notion of "object" a bit too intensively to think about and describe architecture. I mean that buildings are very rarely objects – if then, eventually a temple or a cathedral, but most buildings are not objects. They still have to do with the city: and when they have to do with the city, the notion of objects is dissolved.

For me, I like to clearly distinguish type as applied to singular objects, isolated buildings ... if related to cities and morphology, then type is something else. There are two different ways of conceiving it. At the time, when we were absorbed in this discussion of types, we wanted to resolve once and for all the issues of how buildings were built and how cities were built. Today, we speak too much in terms of how buildings stand by themselves. And yet the notion of types is still valuable.

I would like to add that I still believe, even in the present circumstances, in the importance of recognising how cities grow, and their value ... we need to pay attention to the discussion of the Sixties, when the notion of type was more "pregnant". However, the notion of type was maybe also interpreted too literally, and this was the burden that actually sank the idea and made type an old-fashioned term that didn't deserve to be recognised any more.

You could take what was done in Italian schools in the Seventies, and even in America, i.e. the Florida school, as examples of what I am thinking about. They interpreted what type meant in a very easy way, in a very superficial way. What you have to keep in mind is that type is a structure that is very inapprehensible.

<u>In your text, you also describe type as something eminently flexible: "a frame where change can happen". And you also refer to the special moment where an architect creates a new type.</u>

New types don't occur so easily. A couple of years ago we were invited to go to the AA [Architectural Association School of Architecture], and we participated in a symposium in 2014 called "Type versus Typology". I was forced to rethink precisely this question. I pointed out three moments, three projects of mine, that it seemed to me had to do with types and where the notion of type was present: the Urumea Residential Building in San Sebastian [with Javier Marquet, Javier Unzurunzaga and also Luis M. Zulaica 1968–1973, Fig. 14]; the project for the Actur de Lacua competition in Vitoria [1977], with Manuel de Solà-Morales [Fig. 15]; and the urban plan for the city of Aranjuez [with Manuel de Solà-Morales, Jean Busquets, Juan José Echeverría & Manuel Salinas, 1981].

<u>Our own interest is in the potential of typological studies as an operative tool in today's design process, meaning beyond the historical process it generates.</u>

I would say that in my current practice the notion of type reappears. No doubt about it. The latest project I'm thinking about is a hotel in Havana. When someone works on a subject like this, type is the appropriate way to deal with the site ... then you will have a typological approach. You will start thinking in terms of hotel rooms, which has to do with bathrooms and the space for sleeping, or other complementary spaces, and so on. A kind of typological thinking starts automatically. Then you will find that many of the subsequent operations are more related to contingency: contingency about site, but also about programmes, means of construction, norms and so on. One needs to think how the corridor will be connected to the elevator, why one locates the elevator in this position, etcetera.

<u>So working with types can be seen as a form of knowledge ...</u>

Yes, I would say so.

Getting back to the moment of invention, when, one, you say that it can come from the transformation of existing types or the fusion of them.

That is the greatest moment of an architect's career, without necessarily making a completely new type. For example, the housing project in San Sebastian, in a very early moment in my life. At the time I didn't know so much about type, and yet typology as an operative tool was present. Unity and continuity in the city block was one of the goals I wanted to achieve. [Moneo starts sketching a drawing to explain the project.] The specificity of this typological solution was obtained through the position of the vertical circulations, elevators and stairs. The typological problem was how to resolve a nineteenth-century housing block in a way that achieved a unity ... the inconvenience was the way the splitting into independent sites had been done. The notion of type can be clearly observed in the project I developed with Manuel de Solà-Morales for the Lacua.

When you come to a project like the intervention for the Thyssen-Bornemisza [1989–1992], I knew something about palace typologies. Even although I respected the façade, I wanted to enter inside the existing perimeter of windows. I was able to do so because I was conscience about the typology, and how it worked. But I wanted a museum that kept the palace-type museum. I didn't replicate the old palace structure: I created a "new palace", keeping the existing façade, the perimeter. I believe the notion of type was present in this design process. The thing that is present in the built "new palace" which holds the Thyssen-Bornemisza Collection is the notion of type I had of how a "palace type museum" works.

The misunderstanding of type in the late Seventies came mostly from this idea of repetition, that somehow had to do with a certain Marxist view, associating, wrongly, architectural repetition with egalitarianism. I would say the concept of type at that time could have been more flexible.

At a certain point in your essay you underline the power of type to transform or to be transformed from a generic content to the specific and unique. Later you criticise Robert Venturi and his Nantucket Island Houses of 1970. You point out that Venturi reduces types to image-types, ignoring the specific types of the American vernacular house at the same time as keeping its image. This breaks a certain unity that one would otherwise expect.

I still think so. Venturi accepts the iconographical image that we associate with the "Nantucket type of house". The only aspect he incorporates into his work is the iconographic one. He's not concerned with the house structure ... something that doesn't imply only the static aspect. In the end, a true typological intervention should be able to work indoors and outdoors. That means working with spaces, the programme and the means of construction simultaneously. That is what Venturi does not do.

You refer to it as a "broken link", and you add a footnote that could have been written today. You say: "Often the typological analysis is used primarily as a term of reference to underscore the virtue of the proposed design." With the volume of images and references one sees now trending throughout contemporary practices, do you think we're in a one-way situation where images-as-type prevail over type-plans, type-functions or other dimensions of typological studies?

I have in mind the cover of a magazine featuring the Fondazione Feltrinelli by Herzog & de Meuron in Milan. This is a clear example of how the notion of the rural house, even with the pitched roof – that in this particular case is not even a roof anymore – is associated with what the building and development regulations allow. How the larger scale of the city works. Not considering it as the result of the addition of small elements. Suddenly, the notion of type reappears.

It has become a current practice to use images of architecture that come from our memories of old types, that are reborn in these unexpected conditions. That has something to do what we mentioned about Venturi. In his case, we don't have the small house any more; instead we have the presence of an image-type that seeks to reassure the memory of old digested types.

Is it a reduction of the potential of type as a design tool to only consider images of types?

What happens is that ... the more buildings don't depend upon construction, the more you're liberated, and you escape from the structure of the building and become removed from the notion of type. When architects no longer depend on technique, more and more buildings become dissociated from the way they are built. Then the only thing that remains is the memory of how those architectures were. Therefore, type will only re-emerge in terms of a figurative and iconographical condition, losing the structure that was once present in all traditional and vernacular architecture. We live in a time in which we need to readjust all of our notions with which we look at and understand cities ... whether we want to serve ourselves or not by using that implicit knowledge. What is the reason to keep old cities alive?

There are certainly economic reasons, but in the end old cities have a value in themselves that cannot be broken. This idea of understanding the relationship between the form of the city and the form of the building intersects with the notion of morphology, and at this moment the issue of typology is valuable and needed. Let me use this example by Herzog & de Meuron again. This can help us to properly identify the different readings of the notion of type. We can all see a lot of buildings where we know quite well how they have been built. One can guess the number of storeys, the partitions, maybe two or four apartments per floor, but in end it is their form that constructs the iconography of the city. Here, in Herzog & de Meuron's project, what we still have is the iconography of the city. In the middle of all of this morphological coherence and the consistency of this part of the city, the project still belongs to it, and to the idea of how types work, even if when you look at the plan you realise they have another intention. The volume respects the alignments of the urban structure, keeping a certain memory, but they approach it with a different structure inside. This example, maybe less literally, still repeats what we discussed relating to Venturi.

<u>This means that the reduction of type to image is not a negative development?</u>

I would see it as a positive strategy. It is joyful, but in other terms. It still ensures the coherence of the city and the continuity of history, and it is less painful than a stricter and orthogonal volume. I would not speak about reduction, just about an alternative approach to the use of type. In the case of Fondazione Feltrinelli, it brings about an unexpected novelty without betraying the memory people have of their city and what it could be. It is a sophisticated way of reading it.

<u>We're also interested in understanding your point of view about typology as a teaching tool.</u>

It is almost impossible not to use it. It's such a synthetic way to solve specific structures within architecture; in order to understand how things work. Nowadays, you also need to apply it to other kinds of associations to describe unexpected typological relations. In other words, type allows you to find common features in the building structure of a Palladian villa and nineteenth-century Berlin courtyards. Even if type doesn't work in the same unitary way as it did in the past, it's still necessary to associate or to establish common relations between buildings that want to be truly independent. Even taking these single pieces of architecture, we're able to find out shared features with other buildings that would allow us to think of type as a still-living concept.

<u>Type therefore ensures inscription in the long line of architectural history.</u>

It's maybe an unbreakable tool. In the end there is the idea of "whole". How could one tolerate the Feltrinelli intervention if it wasn't for its iconographic dress? Without being offensive. It's a matter of an astute strategy, and this takes us back to the iconographic use of the notion of type. There are image-types as well as structural-types. I'm coming back to where this part of the conversation began. You mentioned Venturi. This was a moment where architecture was identified with the image itself, and this is clearly the case again. The architect says, "I'm going to be forgiven by the fact that I am proposing a solution that works with the city." Without the iconographic presence of type it would be easy to transform their project into a straightforward and less city-related solution. The Fondazione Feltrinelli intervention doesn't deny the city completely. Instead, they're protected by the memory of this "pitched-roof"-type volume.

<u>If we work with images, we are also working with types …</u>

We need to go back to the meaning of "whole". The whole is so much more satisfactory if it involves many more different aspects of the building, and not only one. Here [in Herzog & de Meuron's project] it is only one. The more the type is able to convey, the better it is. They are doing that very often, for example the museum in Berlin [the winning project for the Neue Nationalgalerie – Museum of the 20th Century]. We can identify the same strategy.

<u>You're right, it seems to be the same strategy … Regarding practices like yours, working in an international field and that are required to jump between different cultural and built contexts, could we say that the knowledge of types is a language like Esperanto?</u>

That is a difficult question. More than Esperanto. I think there are many languages, but not a single language anymore. We are able to accept many more languages than a single one. But that is only half-true. Even in the world, everyone is trying to speak a *lingua franca* like English is. You don't enjoy language any more. That would be the answer. We are not looking for an Esperanto anymore, even though we need it.

Chapter 5

Steal Schinkel

Karl Friedrich Schinkel's Bauakademie is without doubt one of the architect's masterpieces and an important part of the Neo-Classical architecture of Berlin. The brief of the design studio proposed the planning of a new academy building that could function mainly as an architectural school and exhibition centre. The goal was to study the idea of tradition and take into account the challenges it poses in terms of renewal and innovation. The proposed projects investigated the relationship between very functional purpose, historical quotation and poetical refinement, taking into account the adjacent urban-renewal projects in Berlin Mitte.

Laboratory EAST   Steal Schinkel   2016

Rather than seeking a faithful reconstruction of the iconic building of the Bauakademie, the intention of the design studio was to find a contemporary interpretation in a manner that Schinkel might have undertaken, and in so doing developing a brief for a new academy building that would serve as both an architecture school and an exhibition centre.

Towards a New Bauakademie

Anja & Martin Fröhlich

Whilst somewhat mischievous, the title "Steal Schinkel" should not dispel the impression that this project concerns what Karl Friedrich Schinkel himself postulated as "the historic and the poetic".[1] The subtitle makes it quite clear what this is about, namely architectural designs for a new Bauakademie. This is a direct reference to Karl Friedrich Schinkel's *Sammlung architektonischer Entwürfe* (1819–40), which constitutes an ideal medium for studying his ideas.[2] Schinkel's approach to architecture was indisputably through the medium of the image — both via his admiration of the drawings of his later teacher Friedrich Gilly and via the drawings he produced himself. It is this mediating role of the image in Schinkel's work that is of particular interest to us: an absorption in how Schinkel thought and designed in scenes and depictions, not just as a painter but also as an architect in his compositional approach to presenting architecture. This aspect of his work is equally evident in his works, each of them driven as they are by a strength of vision.[3]

This powerful emotive effect of images plays a central role in our project idea. For us, the practice of architectural design is also a process of producing images and a means of articulating visions. Discourse on architecture is also a discourse on images conducted using images. Paradoxically perhaps, this is similarly visible in the debate surrounding the fate of Schinkel's lost Bauakademie, where the core arguments revolve around an idealised depiction from the past.

Background

Schinkel's Bauakademie, built from 1832 to 1836, is unquestionably one of the architect's masterpieces. The term "Bauakademie" actually refers to two things: on the one hand, the building; and on the other, the institution that it housed, it being originally and first and foremost an academy for architects and engineers. Only later was this meaning eclipsed by the aura of the building itself, which acquired an iconic status in the history of German architecture for its uniqueness. Situated self-assuredly as a stand-alone building next to the Berliner Stadtschloss, it was the first secular building in Prussia to feature exposed brickwork. Taking his cue from early British factory buildings, Schinkel reinterpreted the cultural tradition of brick architecture here in northern Germany to produce a building that ran contrary to the prevailing tendencies of the time. In terms of its plan, it is perhaps the most rigorous example of a quadratic building typology. As a hybrid building, it united several functions under one roof. Sales areas for the Royal Porcelain Manufactory or the court jeweller on the ground floor linked it to the daily life of the surrounding city. The first floor was used by the Building Academy, and comprised lecture halls and drawing ateliers, workrooms for the teaching staff and a library, all linked by broad corridors. The second floor housed the seat of the Prussian Building Authority, together with Schinkel's residence and atelier. An archive on the upper floor held the records of the building authority. In view of the fact that these quadratic floor plans had to serve a variety of purposes, they had to be flexible, making the customary solution of placing load-bearing walls on top of one another impractical. Schinkel resolved this issue by creating a series of tensioned vaulted ceilings supported by a system of brick pillars, in turn connected by arches to form a framework. By this means, the entire building could dispense with load-bearing walls and, consequently, the different floors could be individually partitioned. As a result, the façade of the building exactly reflects the building's inner structure. Schinkel extended this principle stringently by formulating all four façades of the building identically, in the process creating a building that not only employed what were radically new industrial construction techniques but simultaneously giving these a deliberate exterior expression.

In terms of posterity, Schinkel's genius resulted in a building that can be interpreted in different ways, thus serving as a model for both modernists and traditionalists alike. What fascinated progressive professionals was its unapologetic rationalism as a grid-plan building. Instead of accentuating its axiality by, for example, articulating the central portal, the division of the façades into eight regular axes on each side emphasised the uniformity of the building. As a consequence, the building has been heralded as a precursor of architectural modernism. Vice versa, traditionalists have praised the qualities of "the historic and the poetic" that in Schinkel's view every building should embody if it were to rise above serving mere trivial purposes. The staircase of the building, for example, was illuminated by a glazed roof that was not visible from outside, providing ample daylight and illuminating the extensive ornaments and decorations in the staircase, as well as in the window reveals. The delicate ornamentation of the inlays in the interior continued on the outside through figurative motifs in the terracotta relief of the façade, which Schinkel designed himself. In so doing, Schinkel underlined the importance he accorded to the articulation of the building over and above its "pure radical abstraction",[4] in particular by according the iconography of the relief panels a symbolic importance. What unites the admirers of the Bauakademie from both architectural camps is their unbroken interest in physically reconstructing the building, ideally as a faithful reproduction of the original. Whether this is driven by a desire to resurrect the former urban form or to reconstruct a lost icon has often become mixed up in the ensuing debates. Nonetheless, the presence of the Bauakademie is not intertwined with a desire for political representation, as has been the case with the Berliner Stadtschloss, meaning that it remains all the more significant for the self-conception of architects.

Perspective

After its partial destruction during the Second World War and the initially declared intention to rebuild it, the Bauakademie was eventually demolished in 1962 to make way for a building for the East German (DDR) Ministry of Foreign Affairs, subsequently constructed in 1965 and itself demolished a mere thirty years later. Since 2004, an imagined replica of the building depicting the exact dimensions of the original has stood on the former site of the historical predecessor. This facsimile is a supposedly authentic reconstruction of a single corner of the building, intended as an ideal demonstration of modern craftsmanship skills and knowledge, and incorporating the most up-to-date reproduction techniques for replica stonework and terracotta panels. The remaining scaffolding around the footprint of the building was clad with printed plastic hoardings that show an exact representation of the former façade and all its details, thereby simulating the presence of the building – as an "entertaining folly" – in the urban realm. What appears outwardly as the illusion of a solid, closed building frontage has inside become a veritable thicket of trees and shrubs growing between the scaffolding, now incongruously serving as a habitat for numerous birds. This stark discrepancy between the overgrown situation within and the pristine pipe dream of the building's reconstruction on the outside inadvertently acts only to portray the spectrum of possibilities for its replacement.

The current condition was the starting point for our 2016 design-studio project Steal Schinkel. Rather than seeking a faithful reconstruction of this iconic building, the intention was to find a contemporary interpretation in a manner that Schinkel might have undertaken, and in so doing developing a brief for a new academy building that would serve as both an architecture school and exhibition centre. In all the designs, we discussed how they might relate to Schinkel. At the same time, we sought solutions that were both technologically innovative and poetic, inspired by the freedom to pose ever-new questions, to probe and to absorb what the newest findings are. These key questions included: How do we deal with the legacy of Schinkel's Bauakademie? How much of Schinkel's substance do we incorporate into the new building? How do we respond to the urban context of the site? How can we accommodate future changes to the building's function and use? How might a contemporary design approach inspired by Schinkel manifest itself – one in which we reference Schinkel, whose architecture itself drew on further references to historical building forms and elements, which he himself remodelled and composed to match his own intentions?

A detailed study of the urban context and the core idea and structure of Schinkel's building was undertaken, involving its various permutations in terms of use and coupled with an analysis of contemporary educational concepts at international architecture schools, following which key design parameters were identified. As a common basis for the design studio, it was decided that all of the proposals should maintain the urban square and the overall size and dimensions of the building as Schinkel originally conceived them. Moreover, the design should be developed around a regular underlying grid that determined the structural system, the floor plans and the articulation of the façades. Lastly, the original flexible-plan idea should be transformed using contemporary means and an innovative construction method.

Each of the designs that emerged can therefore be seen as a statement proposing a contemporary interpretation of the Bauakademie in the spirit of Schinkel rather than a reconstruction of Schinkel's original. In reference to the culture of the image, a perspective visualisation of each project was made from the same standpoint that Schinkel originally took for his *Collected Architectural Designs*, chosen as a means of mediating between the image of the original and its contemporary reinterpretation. Each design forms a hypothetical proposition that attempts to embody the memory of Schinkel's ideas, to translate them into the present and to reinterpret them in the context of modern-day requirements and technical capacities. And each project thus strives to establish a relationship between functional purpose, historical reference and poetic finesse. Most importantly, common to them all is the express intention not to attempt to recreate a masterpiece from the past.

1 Karl Friedrich Schinkel, *Das Architektonische Lehrbuch*, ed. Goerd Peschken (Berlin: Deutsche Kunstverlag, 1979), p. 150.

2 Published (in English as Karl Friedrich Schinkel, *Collected Architectural Designs* (London & New York: Academy Editions/ St. Martin's Press, 1982).

3 The Altes Museum in Berlin, for example, with its broad stairs, gives the visitor the impression of standing eye-to-eye with the monarch in the Stadtschloss opposite. Equally, the most pronounced aspect of Friedrichswerder Church is of its inner buttresses that step back to allow the gallery to be placed above them, unlike most churches of the day where massive buttresses were typically arranged as an exterior element.

4 Schinkel, *Das Architektonische Lehrbuch*, p. 150.

Scale 1:750

Kimberley Berney & Andrea Ishii

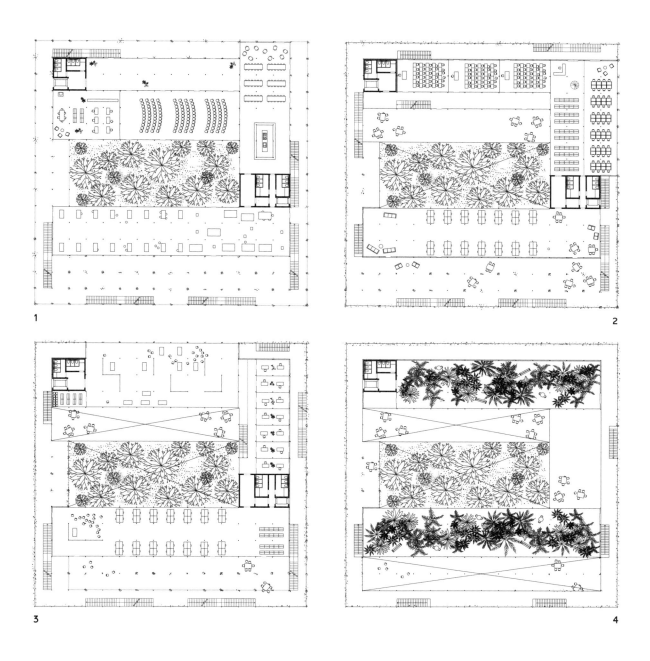

Laboratory EAST   Steal Schinkel

363

Francesca Bianchi & Jérémy Prongué

Scale 1:750

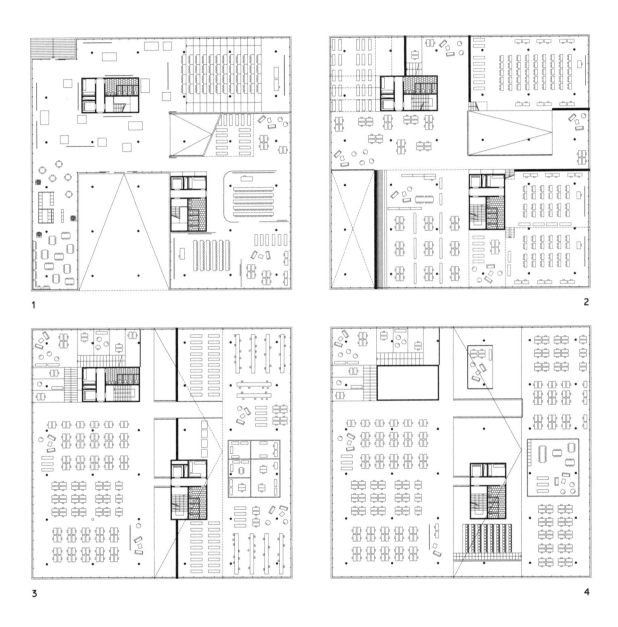

1

2

3

4

Scale 1:750

Valentine Compain & Constance Steinfels

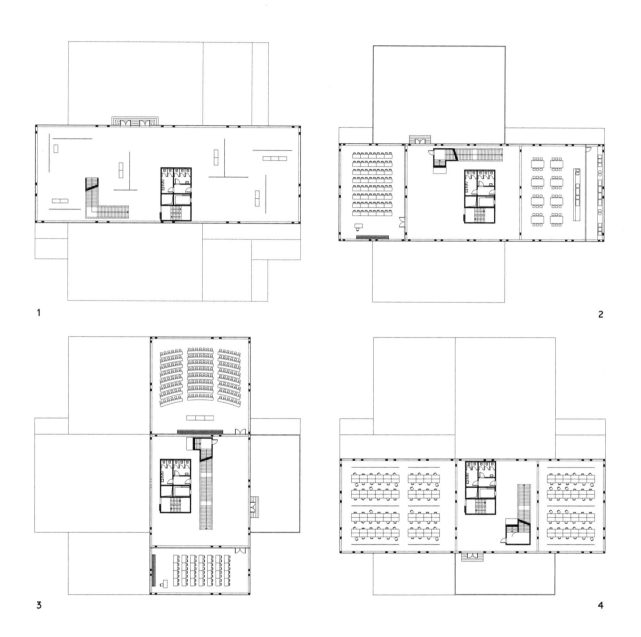

Laboratory EAST   Steal Schinkel

Enrico Chizzolini & Elodie Dias

Scale 1:750

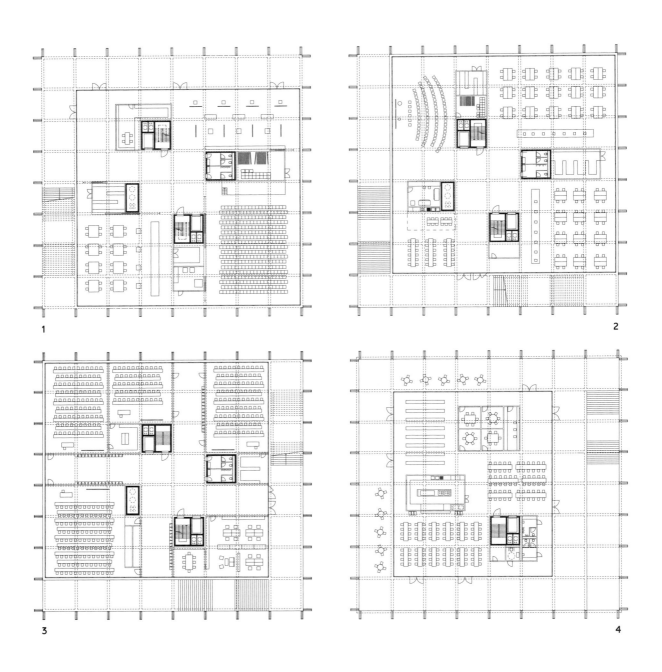

368   Steal Schinkel   Laboratory EAST

Scale 1:750   Julie Crot & Nicolas Rychner

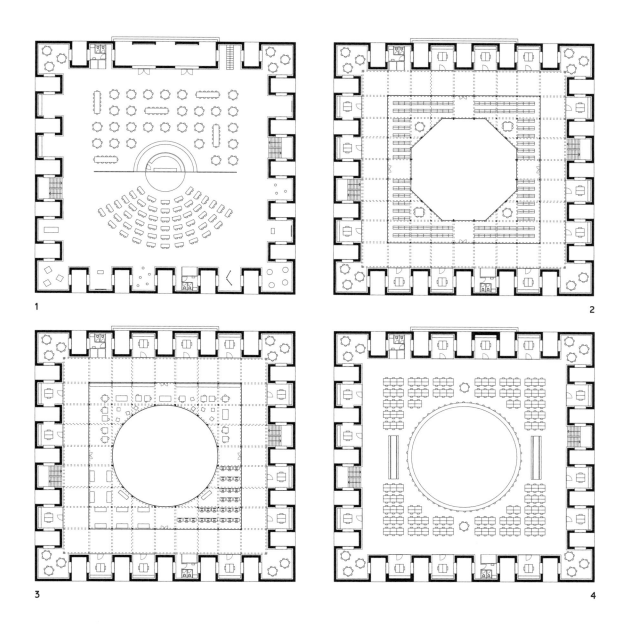

Darine Dandan & Soukaïna Richard

Scale 1:750

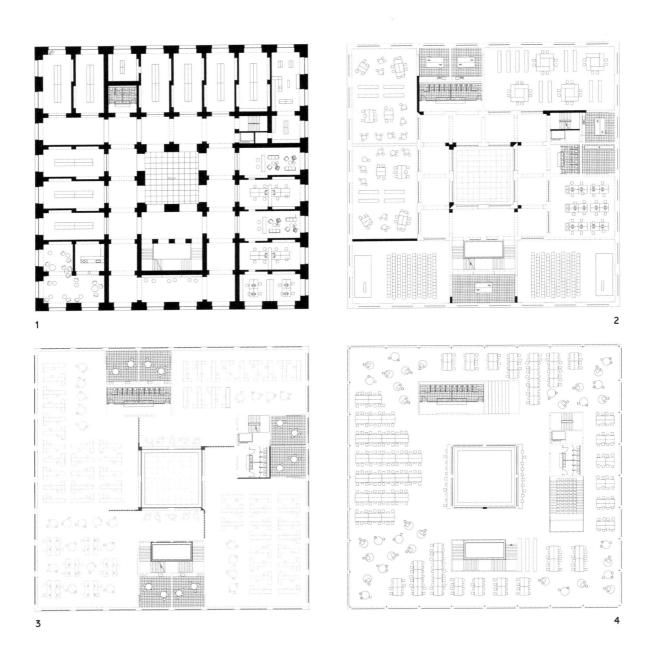

1
2
3
4

Steal Schinkel   Laboratory EAST

Scale 1:750

Grégory D'Antonio & Houssam Ben Hallam

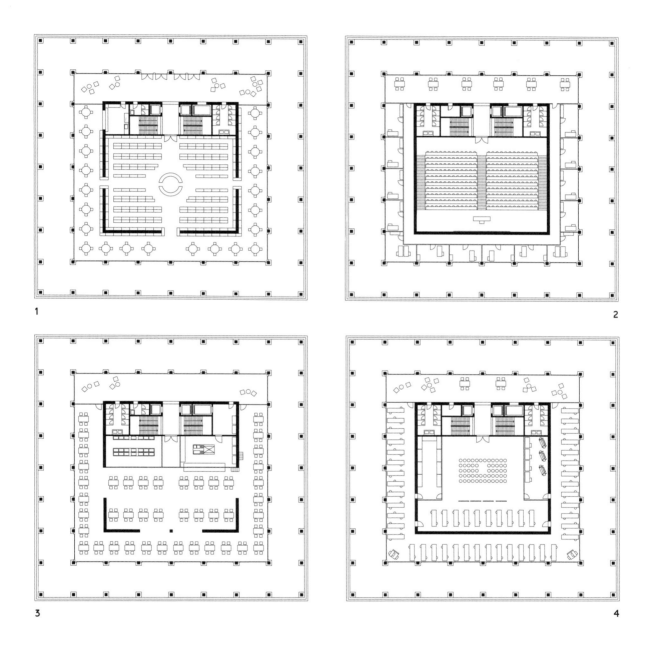

Laboratory EAST   Steal Schinkel

375

Emilien Ducommun & Maseeh Takhtravanchi

Scale 1:750

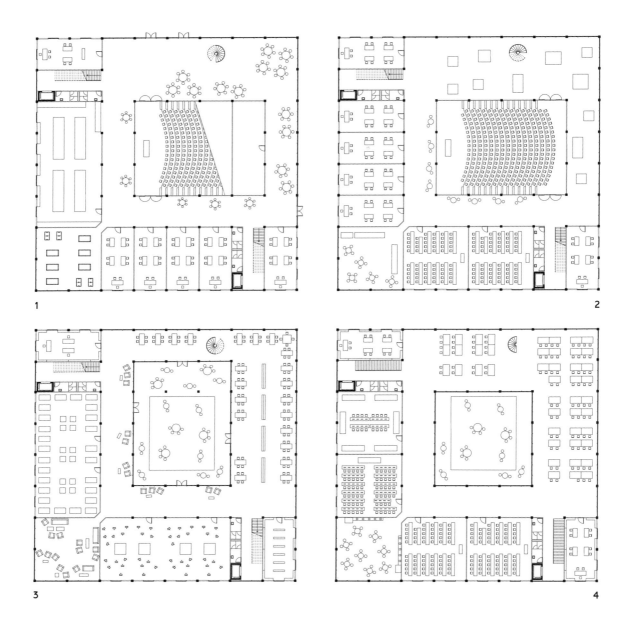

1

2

3

4

Scale 1:750

Florent Dubois & Daniela Lopes

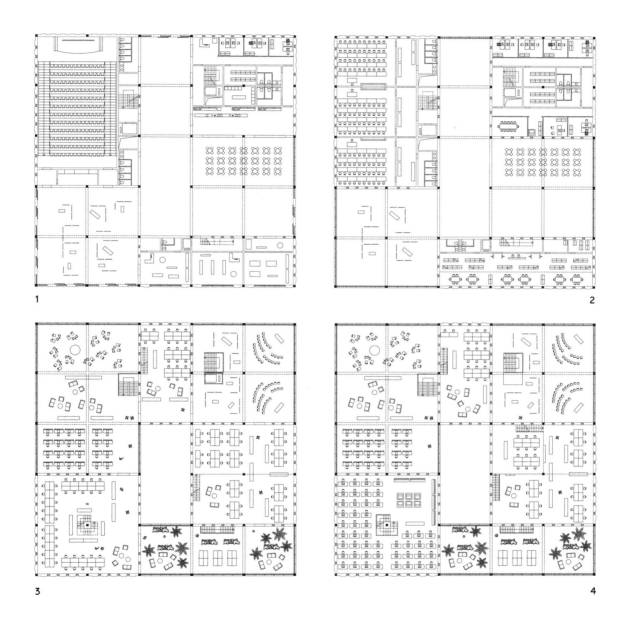

Laboratory EAST   Steal Schinkel

Aude Faure & Siying Li

Scale 1:750

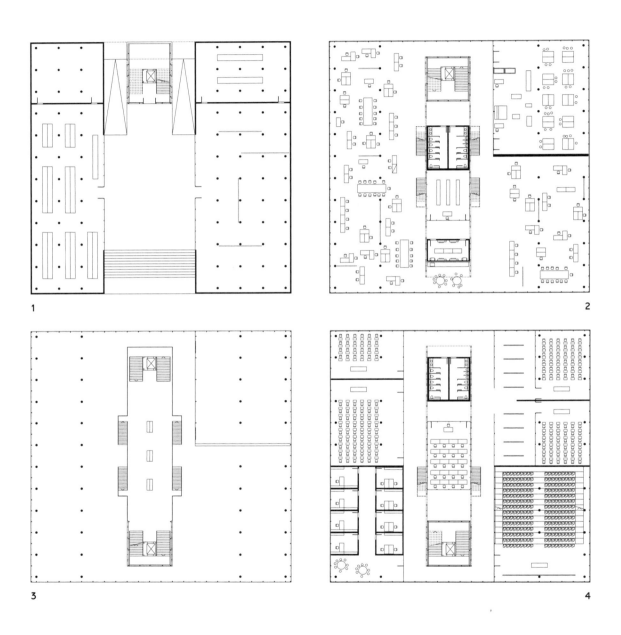

1

2

3

4

380 Steal Schinkel Laboratory EAST

Scale 1:750

Anne-Claire Gandor & Quentin Huegi

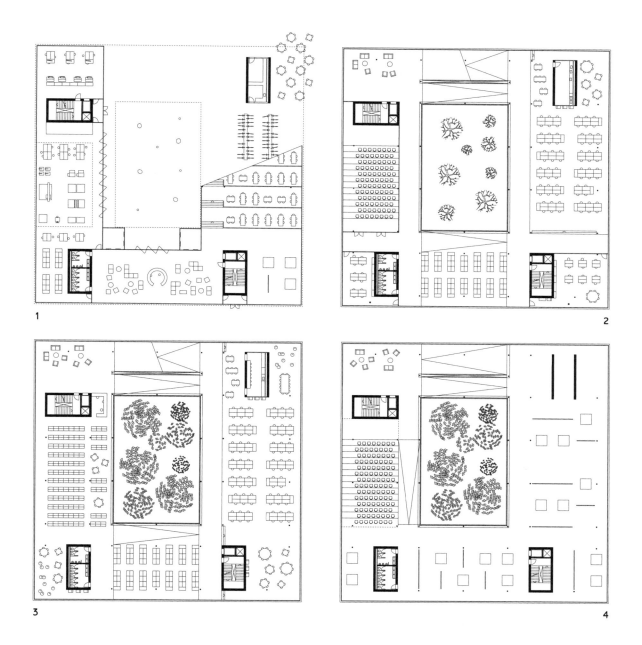

Laboratory EAST   Steal Schinkel

383

Omar Imadiouni & Chujun Zong

Scale 1:750

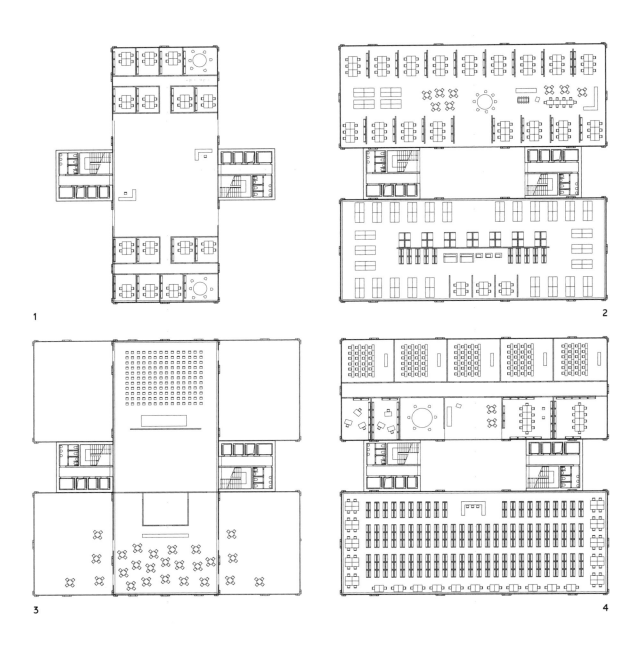

1
2
3
4

Scale 1:750

Valentine Jacques & Florence Nyffeler

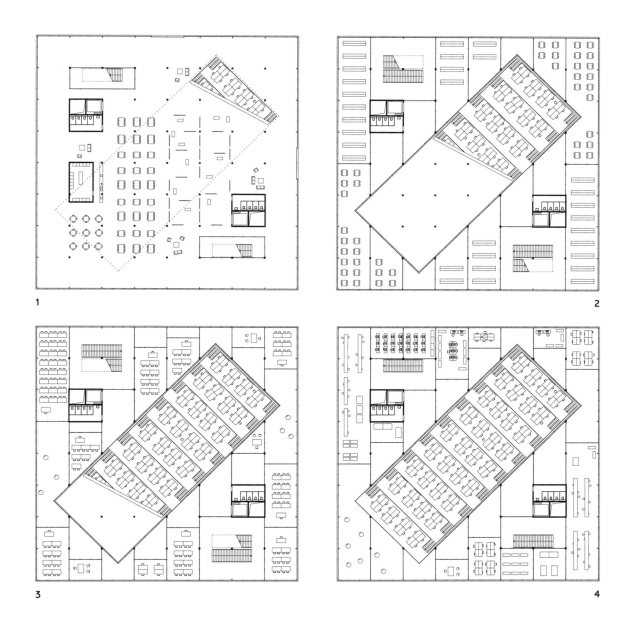

1

2

3

4

Laboratory EAST   Steal Schinkel

387

Yasmine El Karmoudi & Marion Moutal

Scale 1:750

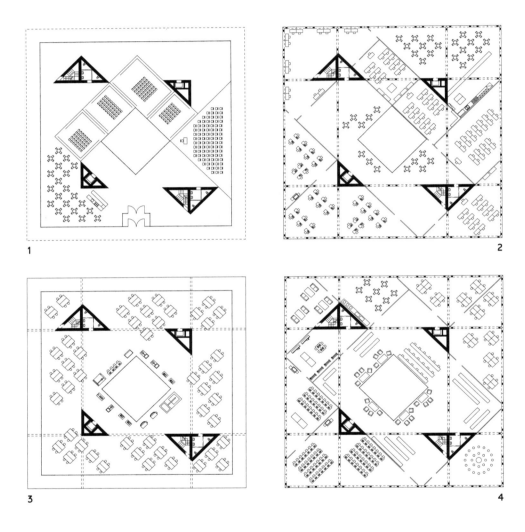

388   Steal Schinkel   Laboratory EAST

Scale 1:750

Younes Louhichi

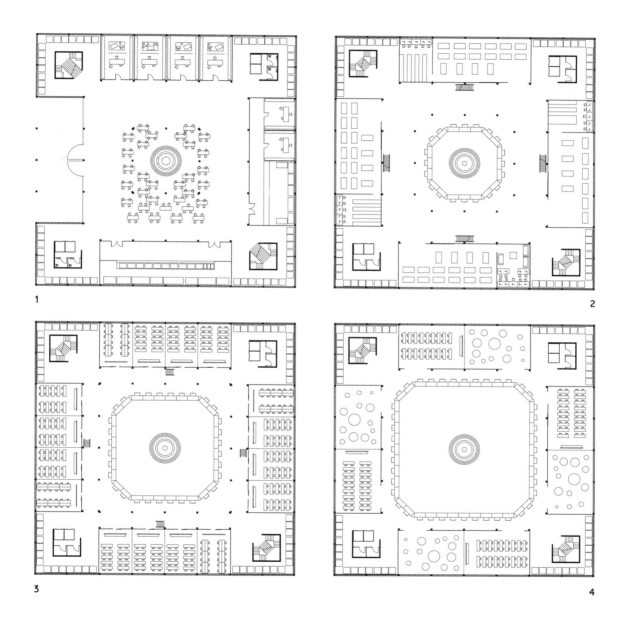

Laboratory EAST   Steal Schinkel

Charlotte Roche-Meredith

Scale 1:750

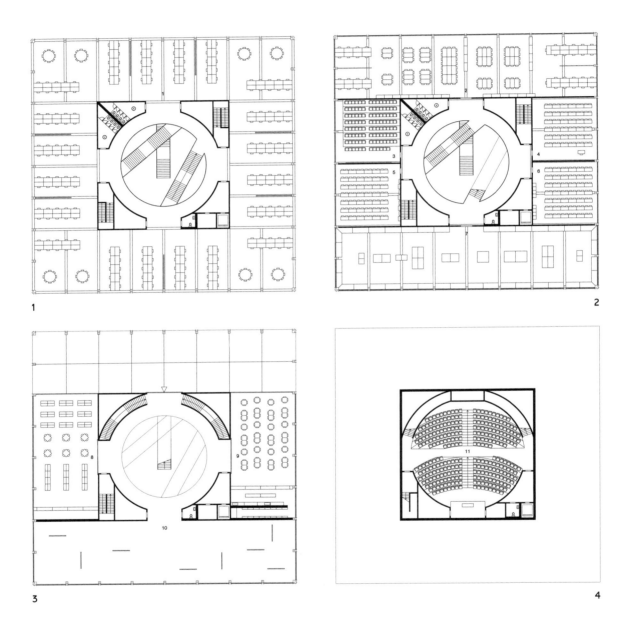

392   Steal Schinkel   Laboratory EAST

Scale 1:750

Arnaud Miguet & Andrea Van

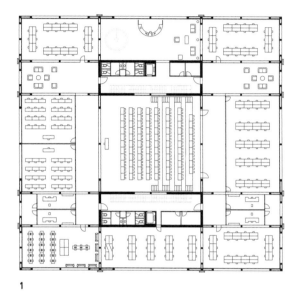

1

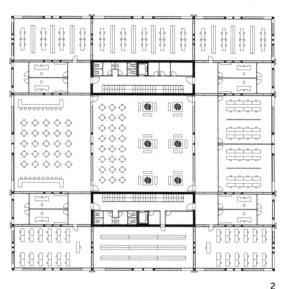

2

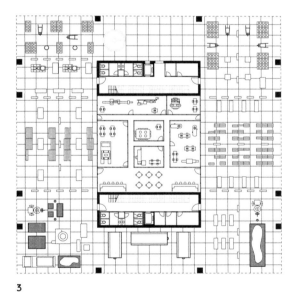

3

Marta De Benito Ortiz & Séverine Routhier

Scale 1:750

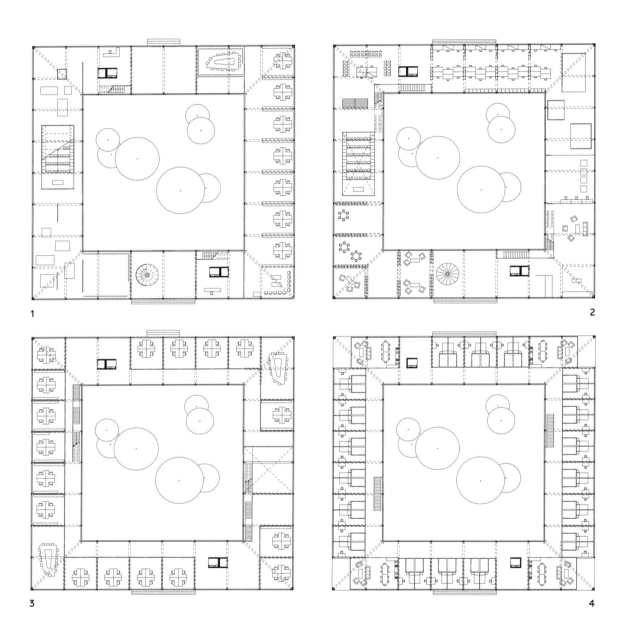

396   Steal Schinkel   Laboratory EAST

Scale 1:750

Maryem Sadek & Salla Sivunen

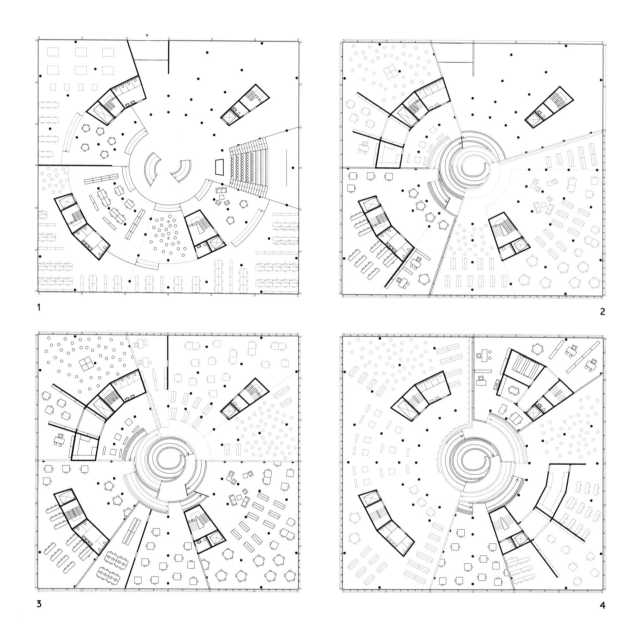

Laboratory EAST — Steal Schinkel

Laurent Soulier

Scale 1:750

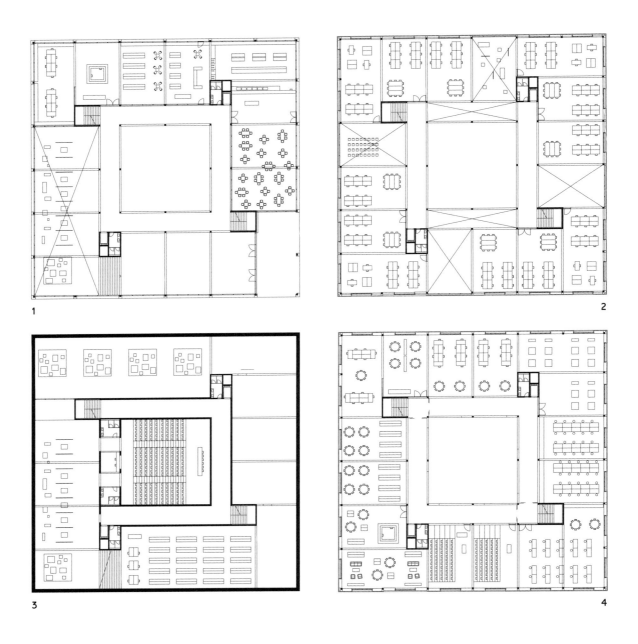

400   Steal Schinkel   Laboratory EAST

Urban Design as Constellation

On the Meaning and Relevance of the Work of Karl Friedrich Schinkel

Roland Züger

The reconstructed Berliner Stadtschloss will soon once again occupy the heart of the German capital. However, without Schinkel's Bauakademie it lacks the carefully composed spatial relationships it once had. Why is the ensemble around the Bauakademie still so admired today? A quest for clues.

For Karl Friedrich Schinkel (1781–1841), the Baroque-style in Berlin was a curse. His designs for the centre of Berlin in the early nineteenth century were intended to spell an end of the rigid block grid and the Baroque excesses of its architecture, along with its narrow-minded spirit. Thus his projects broke with the block structure, taking the form of almost landscape-like arrangements of building volumes, an approach that was entirely new at the time. These precisely placed structures, and the Bauakademie (1831–1836) in particular, entered into a dynamic dialogue with the other buildings in their surroundings — a concept of creating urban constellations that established sets of open spatial relationships. This order was rooted in a new understanding of space that arose, on the one hand, out of a range of scientific and scholarly discoveries in the early industrial period, and, on the other, out of an awareness of the need to adapt the city to the needs of the rising middle classes.

This breakthrough (quite literally) in the comprehension of space can still be sensed today when walking along the boulevard Unter den Linden from the Pariser Platz to the Museumsinsel. As one approaches the Humboldt University and the Opera, the "Rue corridor" begins to widen, as if being allowed to breathe. Passing over the Schlossbrücke (1821–4) – likewise designed by Karl Friedrich Schinkel – one enters the so-called landscape of the Kupfergraben. Here one can see the course of the River Spree along what was once the Kupfergraben canal. The view spans from where Schinkel's Bauakademie stood, over the bridge to the Berliner Schloss, to Schinkel's Altes Museum (1825–30) and on past the tax-authority building in the direction of the Packhof (1830–2) to the warehouses that Schinkel had conceived in 1829 to cater for the rise in freight trade along the river.

Rather than completely reconfiguring the area, Schinkel's creation of a new spatial conception lay in the precise placement of individual buildings. The following sections detail the central characteristics of his strategy: the placement of stand-alone buildings, the negation of frontality, the deployment of spatially defining corners, and ultimately Schinkel's understanding of space as landscape.

Schinkel's intense dislike of the predominantly uniform Baroque image of Berlin at the time did not stop short of the various royal buildings, several of which he more than once proposed remodelling or demolishing. In 1816, Schinkel found only the Schloss and the armoury worth preserving.

As the Prussian state's financial coffers would not stretch to that, Schinkel elected instead to use the transformative capacity of individual buildings to adapt the city, undertaking only selective interventions in the urban realm.

The plans for Friedrichswerder, which included Schinkel's Bauakademie and Friedrichswerder Church (1824–30), offer an illuminating example of how, through the placement of an "entirely freestanding building on a square footprint with four identical elevations",[1] the architect's design for the Bauakademie triggered a reordering of the wider surroundings. In order to do so, the building first had to be "liberated from the unsightly old rearward buildings",[2] a sentiment that still rings true today given the assorted medley of new buildings that have since sprung up there in the name of restoring the city's historical plan.

As his proposal for the Friedrichswerder Church show, for Schinkel any means were justified in order to accentuate the urban presence of his buildings, in this particular case going as far as to screen off his building from its immediate environment using freestanding walls and trees. Although he invariably had to incorporate the buildings of his predecessors in his concepts, Schinkel's projects are frequently freestanding objects. They acquire three-dimensionality through the dialectic between the built object and urban space. In the case of the Bauakademie and the Altes Museum, the edges of Schinkel's buildings are thrust forward into the urban space of the Kupfergraben, directing attention away from the centre of the façade elevation to the corner of the building volume.

A revealing example of this approach stood until 1905 on Pariser Platz: the Palais Redern (1828–30), which Schinkel extensively remodelled. The old original building occupied a prominent corner site – on which the Hotel Adlon now stands – and was a typical example of an elegant Baroque town house. Schinkel added a third storey in place of the former mansard roof and sacrificed the Baroque character of the façades in favour of Florentine-style elevations modelled on those of Palazzo Pitti. In so doing, Schinkel consciously introduced the new style of the Neo-Renaissance – as Leo von Klenze (1784–1864) had also done in Munich – into the late Baroque street elevations of Unter den Linden. The new building made no attempt to blend into its surroundings; indeed it contrasted markedly with them. In an assessment that Schinkel wrote about his own design in his capacity as director of the State Construction Commission, he noted that "in our view, the beauty of the Pariser Platz is in no way compromised by the addition of a third storey to the residence of Count Redern. On the contrary, we are of the opinion that it would be a blessing for the square when at some point the very ugly mansard roofs were to be removed."[3] Schinkel was highly critical of the forced uniformity that compelled people to live in identical living conditions. Aside from a larger degree of individual expression and plurality, Schinkel's goal in breaking with stylistic conformity was also to achieve a greater general diversity in the volumetric composition of buildings.

With the Palais Redern, the corner of the Pariser Platz became, so to speak, the new centrepoint of the residence. The Palais was no longer arranged around its main axis and the central portal (as its neighbours on the street were), thus according it a greater prominence as a distinct volume in terms of its surroundings. The heightening of the corner at the transitional point where the boulevard meets the square also underlines Schinkel's understanding of how urban presence influences urban space.

This principle is used to particular effect in the Bauakademie, with its identical façades on all sides, whereby a sense of directionality is only apparent in the floor plan. In his etching of the building, Schinkel omits the short flight of steps to the square in front – and with it a possible indication of symmetry – thereby heightening the effect of the rectangular volume. Nothing was allowed to detract from the overall impact of the rectangular, slightly flattened cuboid form. It is the same with the nearby Altes Museum, where even the dome over the central space is obliged to bow to this principle so as to make it invisible when seen from outside.

Corners that define space

Aside from his aversion to what he considered as the overly orderly urban realm of the Baroque, Schinkel's understanding of spatial relationships was also informed to no small degree by his artistic training. Long before he came to work on larger commissions as an architect, he had devoted his time to painting. He produced his first cycle of paintings in 1807, and in 1808 he drew a circular panorama of Palermo[4] that would contribute to popularising veduta painting. His depiction of Palermo shows the city that he visited on his journey to Italy, but in an idealised way. As a painter, Schinkel very much worked in the Romantic tradition. He painted Gothic domes silhouetted against the setting sun, or ruins in the Margraviate of Brandenburg, but he would ultimately become most famous for his painted stage sets.

It was, however, one of his successors, the painter Eduard Gärtner (1801–77), who in the Biedermeier period first overcame the idealised architectural painting style of the time and developed a realistic style devoid of tones of false pathos. And so it transpired that none other than Gärtner the painter would later portray the works of Schinkel the architect.

In this sense, Gärtner's six-part panorama from 1834 – painted from the viewpoint of the roof of Friedrichswerder Church – manages to unite both architecture and painting.[5] In the foreground, the Bauakademie has not been omitted, although not quite finished, and even the scaffolding is recorded in the painting. One can already see how its clearly delineated form defines the surrounding urban realm. Schinkel's own copperplate etchings have a similarly fascinating pictorial quality: his building volumes shift into the frame like stage sets in a theatre, guiding the viewer's eye into the deepness of the spaces.

In the same way that the planets in a solar system maintain different distances to its sun, the buildings in Berlin maintain a balance around an imaginary centre of gravity, which is the Schlossbrücke, around which circle the Altes Museum with the Berlin Cathedral, the Schloss and the Armoury on an inner orbit, and the Bauakademie and Packhof on an outer orbit.[6]

A central means of heightening a sense of depth is to articulate the corners of a building, and Schinkel devotes particular attention to their architectonic elaboration. This is what defines the physical impact and the presence of his buildings. It is not just Schinkel's mastery of details, for instance the incorporation of trivial aspects such as roof drainage into the shadow line of the pilasters, that contributes to this. The articulation of the corner is also a defining factor in the perceived scale of a building, and one that already unfolds its impact from a distance: for example through large orders, as introduced for the Schauspielhaus, or freestanding rows of columns framed by containing walls, such as in the Altes Museum.

City as landscape

Schinkel lived in an era when cities had not yet been encircled by a steadily more built-up hinterland, as would later occur at the height of industrialisation. In Schinkel's time, Berlin was still a pre-industrial city, and a young one at that. On his journey to England with the Prussian statesman Peter Beuth in 1826, however, Schinkel encountered early examples of such extensive urban landscapes and made drawings that anticipated the developments that would later also befall Berlin. The rapid rise in population and expansion of the city's footprint had a disruptive effect on its face and form, and industrialisation – be it the dramatic changes in the economy and political power or the introduction of new means of public transport – had a huge impact on conditions. Such drastic transformations would inevitably make it necessary to develop new ideas of architectural and urban design.

Schinkel's response was the concept of an urban landscape for Berlin. His idea of an open spatial correspondence of building volumes that together form ensembles was, however, limited to the centre of the city.

Aside from the impressions of the big city that Schinkel and Beuth brought back with them from England to Berlin, another source for this new idea of the loose placement of built volumes in space was undoubtedly the emergence of the English landscape garden. The free, no-longer-axial relationships between buildings in the urban realm, the consideration of views from different directions and the succession of paths are very similar to the compositional principles of the landscape garden. The guiding principle in the landscape garden of the era was the attempt to translate pictorial compositions into spatial settings, and Schinkel's first career as a painter would at least suggest that he did not discount pictorial composition in the design of his architectural works.

Schinkel presented his idea of an "unbounded urban space"[7] as an inner-city landscape composed of a number of different urban scenes, for example the ample view from the vestibule of the Altes Museum. This urban loggia was conceived as a place within the building that afforded a panorama of the entire surroundings. Visitors to the Altes Museum could wander back and forth, eye-to-eye as it were with the monarch in the Berliner Schloss on the opposite side of the Lustgarten. Like the architecture of freestanding buildings, this ennobling of urban space in the city was conceived for the then burgeoning middle classes, and thus reveals a political impetus behind Schinkel's work.

Schinkel's idea of the standalone building as a strategy of minimal intervention is no less relevant today. His approach of anchoring buildings dialectically in the urban realm, of emphasising the constellation rather than the solitary building, is, however, challenging in present-day terms. In Schinkel's model, the open spaces between the buildings are just as important as the built elements placed in them. Today, however, this is all too often neglected. Only when urban design thinks in terms of ensembles, in terms of constellations, will it acquire the capacity to develop the strong collective impetus needed to translate our social needs into space.

What this ideal perhaps could potentially mean is embodied, for example, in the scene depicted in Schinkel's stage set for the opening of the Schauspielhaus on Gendarmenmarkt in 1821: the visitors look through an imaginary window out onto a square, standing as a citizen in the middle amidst a constellation of different buildings — an anti-hierarchical spatial conception as a reflection of socio-political emancipation.

---

1   Cited in Tilmann Buddensieg, "Bildungsstadt und Arbeitsstadt", in Hans Kollhoff & Fritz Neumeyer (eds.) *Großstadtarchitektur: City-Achse Bundesallee – Sommerakademie für Architektur, Berlin 1987* (Berlin: Gebr. Mann Verlag, 1989), pp. 25–32, here p. 28. The literature on Schinkel is extensive and continually expanding. Two publications of particular note are Eva and Helmut Börsch-Supan's account of Schinkel's life's work, published by the Deutscher Kunstverlag Berlin and extending to 22 volumes so far, and Jonas Geist, *Karl Friedrich Schinkel: Die Bauakademie – Eine Vergegenwartigung* (Frankfurt a.M.: Fischer, 1993).

2   Cited in Buddensieg, "Bildungsstadt und Arbeitsstadt", p. 28.

3   Cited in Tilmann Buddensieg, " 'Bauen wie man wolle...': Schinkels Vorstellungen der Baufreiheit", *Daidalos*, 7 (1983), pp. 93–103, here p. 95.

4   A detailed discussion of this work can be found in Tilo Eggeling, "Das Panorama von Palermo von 1808", in Helmut Börsch-Supan and Lucius Grisebach (eds.), *Karl Friedrich Schinkel: Architektur, Malerei, Kunstgewerbe*, (Berlin: Verwaltung der Staatlichen Schlösser und Gärten, 1981), pp. 227–8; and Georg Friedrich Koch, "Karl Friedrich Schinkel und die Architektur des Mittelalters: Die Studien auf der erste Italienreise und ihre Auswirkungen", *Zeitschrift für Kunstgeschichte*, 29 (1966), pp. 177–222, here pp. 200–1.

5   Eduard Gärtner also painted further iconic depictions of the centre of Berlin, most notably his portrayal of the Bauakademie (1868) and his view from the Wache to the Berliner Schloss (1849). In his paintings showing the view over the Kupfergraben canal to the dome of the Berliner Schloss beyond, one can see in the background that at the time the row of houses on Schlossfreiheit obscured the view from the Bauakademie to the Berliner Schloss.

6   Andreas Reidemeister, "Städtebau in Berlin: Die Zeit Schinkels und exemplarische Momente bis heute", in Senat von Berlin (ed.), *Karl Friedrich Schinkel: Werk und Wirkung* (Berlin: Nicolaische Verlagsbuchhandlung, 1981), pp. 13–34, here p. 25.

7   Fritz Neumeyer, "Berliner Klassizismus: Der entgrenzte Stadtraum", in Michael Mönninger (ed.), *Das Neue Berlin: Baugeschichte und Stadtplanung der deutschen Hauptstadt* (Berlin: Insel Verlag, 1991), pp. 97–107.

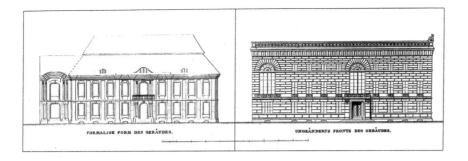

K. F. Schinkel, Palais Kameke-Redern, 1835: (left) elevation of the old Baroque building; (right) the façade of Schinkel's design.

Pariser Platz and the avenue Unter den linden with the Palais Redern. Lithograph c.1840.

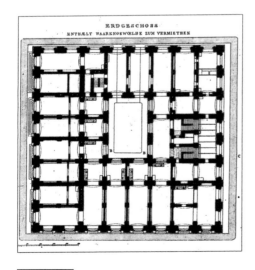

K. F. Schinkel, Allgemeine Bauschule (Bauakademie) Berlin, 1835. Ground-floor plan.

K. F. Schinkel, Friedrich-Werdersche Kirche, Berlin, 1824. Pencil drawing.

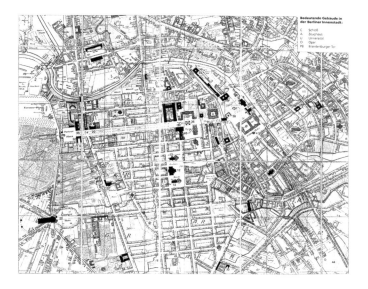

City-centre plan,
Berlin, 1817.

K. F. Schinkel, Neuer Packhof,
Berlin, 1829.

K. F. Schinkel, Altes Museum,
Berlin, 1831.

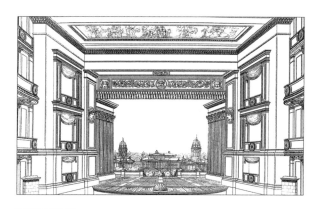

K. F. Schinkel, Schauspielhaus,
Berlin, 1826.

Laboratory EAST   Steal Schinkel

The Agricultural Research Centre in Saint-Aubin, designed by Jakob Zweifel and Heinrich Strickler and built between 1967 and 1970, stands as a remarkable example of Swiss industrial architecture. The complex was used as a research facility until 2016, when it was decommissioned. Using a segment of the site that was economically valueless and earmarked by the local authorities for demolition, EAST designed and built a new temporary art pavilion from reused building elements. The intentions underlying the design can be summed up as an awareness of materials, a pragmatism in approach, and straightforward detailing yet labour-intensive craftsmanship.

Traverse Art Pavilion

Photographs
Joël Tettamanti &
Karsten Födinger

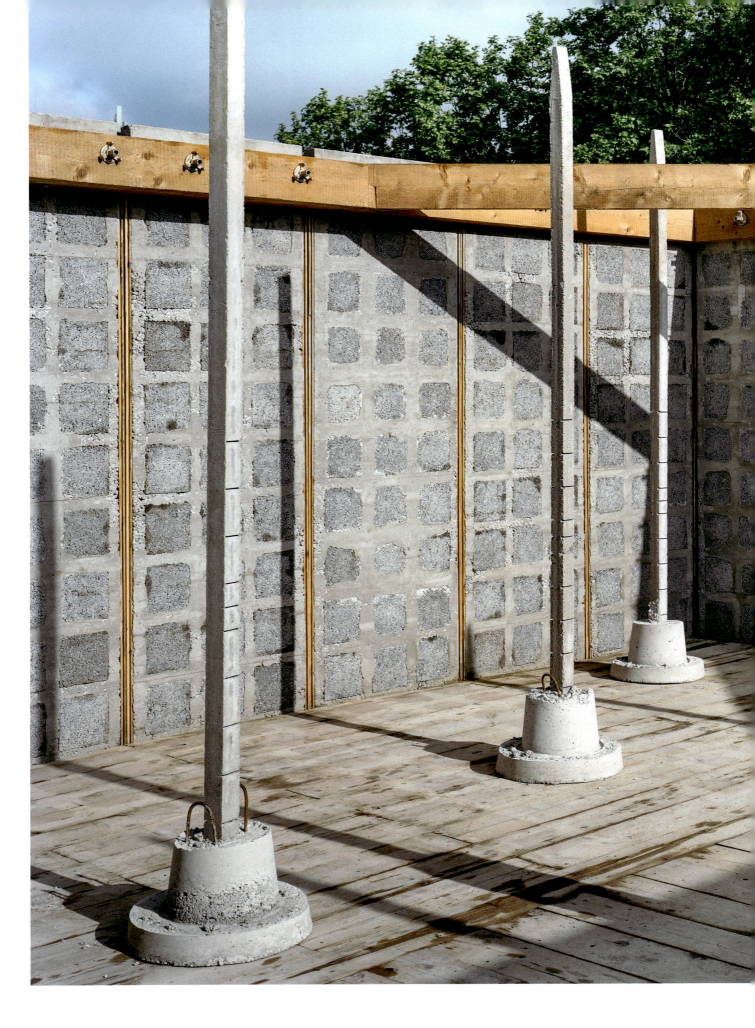

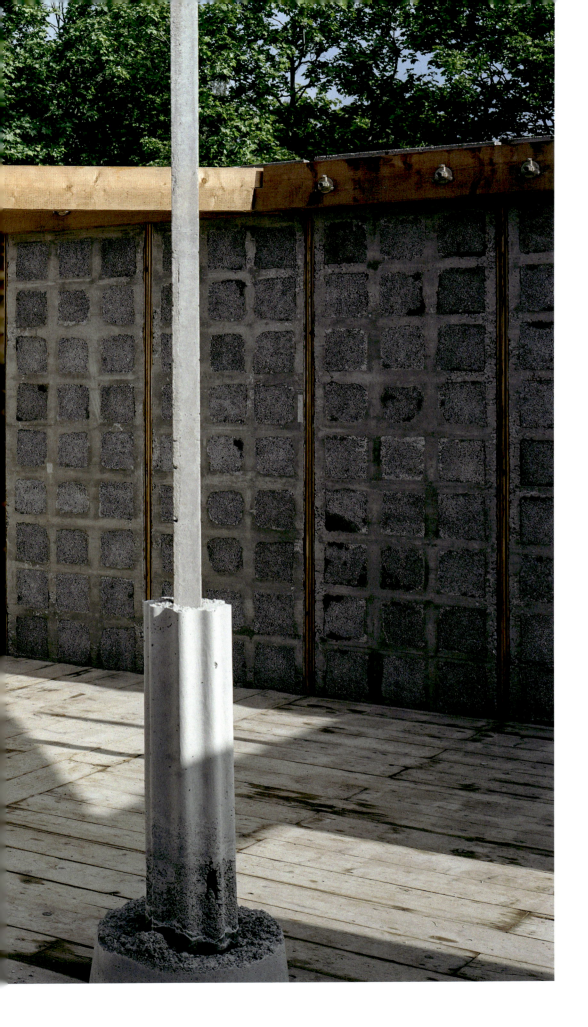

Traverse Art Pavilion   Laboratory EAST

About Editors, Authors, Partners & Students

Editors & Authors

We would like to express our great thanks to the authors and editors, whose research and insight have given this book additional intellectual rigour and substance.

Antje Bittorf: Architect, based in Lausanne. After studying architecture at the Bauhaus-Universität Weimar and TU Delft, she worked from 2006 to 2013 for Staab Architekten in Berlin. From 2012 to 2016 she was a teaching assistant at Laboratory EAST at École Polytechnique Fédérale de Lausanne (EPFL) and now works as an architect in the office Burckhardt+Partner AG in Lausanne. ▸pp.138–43

Tiago P. Borges: Architect and researcher, based in Lausanne. He graduated from the Department of Architecture of the University of Coimbra. He also studied at the École Polytechnique Fédérale de Lausanne (EPFL). Since 2005 he has written about architecture for different media. In 2015 he joined Laboratory EAST at EPFL as a teaching assistant. In 2016 he was distinguished with the Emerging Architecture Critic Award "Erstling" by the Swiss journal *werk, bauen + wohnen*.
▸pp.4–7, 12, 24, 99, 100–1, 144, 156, 288, 301, 302–3, 352–5, 356

Anja Fröhlich: Architect and Doctor of Engineering Sciences (Bauhaus-Universität Weimar). She was appointed Professor of Architecture and Design at the School of Architecture, Civil and Environmental Engineering at École Polytechnique Fédérale de Lausanne (EPFL) in 2012, where she directs Laboratory EAST at the Institute of Architecture. She combines her academic work with architectural practice as part of AFF Architekten in Berlin.
▸pp.26–9, 158–63, 234–7, 358–61

Martin Fröhlich: Architect, based in Berlin. He was appointed Professor of Architecture and Design at the School of Architecture, Civil and Environmental Engineering at École Polytechnique Fédérale de Lausanne (EPFL) in 2012, where he directs Laboratory EAST at the Institute of Architecture. In 2011 he was a Visiting Professor at Berlin University of the Arts (UdK). He co-founded AFF Architekten in Berlin in 1999, which he runs together with Sven Fröhlich. ▸pp.158–63, 234–7, 352–5, 358–61

Sebastian F. Lippok: Studied architecture at Berlin University of the Arts (UdK), and today runs the architectural office WALDRAP in Zurich, together with Renate Walter. From 2013 to 2018 he was a teaching assistant at Laboratory EAST at the École Polytechnique Fédérale de Lausanne (EPFL).
▸pp.144–55

Rafael Moneo: Architect and theoretician. His practical activity includes many museums and cultural spaces. Moneo taught at many universities, finally as professor of Architecture at Harvard University Graduate School of Design. His writings have been published in numerous professional magazines. Moneo has been awarded numerous distinctions, among them the Pritzker Prize for Architecture in 1996 and the Royal Gold Medal of Royal Institute of British Architects in 2003. ▸pp.336–51, 352–5

Marie Theres Stauffer: Architectural historian, based in Geneva. She presently holds an appointment as an Associate Professor of Architectural History at Unité d'histoire de l'art at the University of Geneva. Her research areas cover early-modern, modern and contemporary architecture, as well as the relationship between early-modern science and art. ▸pp.284–7

Joël Tettamanti: Photographer based in Lausanne. He is established as a commercial and media photographer for clients such as Wallpaper*, Kvadrat and several international architects. His work has been featured in solo and group exhibitions in Europe, and has been the subject of several publications, including *Local Studies* (2007), *Davos* (2009) and the monographic book *Works 2001–2019* (2014). Some of his works are part of important art collections such as MUDAM, Villa Noailles, Swiss Foundation of Photography and the Swiss Confederation Art Collection. In 2017, Joël Tettamanti was distinguished with the Prix Culture Photographie BCV of the Fondation Vaudoise pour la Culture.
▸pp.12–23, 288–99, 408–19

Klaus-Dieter Weiß: Architect, art historian and photographer. He taught at the institute of Architecture and Design at the former Technical University Hannover from 1979 to 1987. Since 1981 he has published numerous works on classic-modern and contemporary architecture. He contributes as a correspondent to several international journals.
▸pp.84–97

Roland Züger: Architect and author. From 2002 to 2004 he was a guest lecturer at F+F School of Art and Media Design in Zurich, and from 2007 design tutor at the Institute of Urban Landscape at the Zurich University of Applied Sciences (ZHAW) Winterthur. Since 2011 he has been an editor at the magazine *werk, bauen + wohnen*. In 2006 he founded his own architecture office in Dresden. Since 2010 he has worked with Florian Kessel in Berlin and Zurich.
▸pp.402–7

Partners

We would like to thank the following collaborators for their expert knowledge and valuable contributions, whether in the form of instructive lectures and discussions or in providing their critical reflections when evaluating the projects.

I Best Room Pavilion

Katharina Hohmann, professor, HEAD, Geneva, Switzerland. Jury

Bruno Marchand, professor, LTH-EPFL, Lausanne, Switzerland. Jury

Aldo Nolli, architect, Durisch +Nolli Architetti, Massagno, Switzerland. Jury

Andrea Stitic, assistant, iBOIS-EPFL, Lausanne, Switzerland. Technical expertise

1 Private City

Angela Deuber, architect, HSLU, Luzern, Switzerland. Jury

Donatella Fioretti, professor, TU Berlin, Germany. Jury

Michael Frahn, carpenter, Carpentry Holzmichel Merzligen, Switzerland. Technical expertise

Hartmut Frank, professor, Hafencity Universität Hamburg, Germany. Jury

Renzo Gregori, product designer, Sarna-Granol AG / Keimfarben AG, Switzerland. Jury

Martin Hofstetter, urban planner, Municipal Authority of Renens, Switzerland. Jury

Martin Hug, lawyer, Advokatur & Notariatsbüro Basel, Switzerland. Lecturer

Tinetta Maestre, geographer, Municipal Authority of Renens, Switzerland. Jury

Götz Menzel, architect, GayMenzel, Monthey, Switzerland. Jury

Luca Pattaroni, professor, LASUR-EPFL, Lausanne, Switzerland. Jury

Kristien Ring, architect, AA Projects, Germany. Lecturer

Peter Cachola Schmal, director of the German Architecture Museum, Frankfurt am Main, Germany. Jury

Cyril Veillon, gallerist, ARCHIZOOM-EPFL, Lausanne, Switzerland. Jury

2 The Best Home

Roger Boltshauser, architect, Boltshauser Architekten, Zurich, Switzerland. Jury

Florian Busch, architect, Florian Busch Architects, Tokyo, Japan. Lecturer

Jochen Eisentraut, architect, Zeidler Partnership Architects, Germany. Lecturer

Lisa Euler, researcher, ETH Studio Basel, Switzerland. Lecturer

Serge Favre, business economist, Migros Vaud, Switzerland. Jury

Tanja Reimer, researcher, ZHAW School of Architecture, Design and Civil Engineering, Switzerland. Lecturer

André Tavares, architect and publisher, Dafne Editora, Porto, Portugal. Jury

II Cabanon Art Pavilion

Dan-Alexis Bolomey, professor, LAST-EPFL, Lausanne, Switzerland. Technical expertise and jury

Caroline Dionne, researcher, ALICE-EPFL, Lausanne, Switzerland. Jury

Piet Eckert, architect, E2A Architects, Zurich, Switzerland. Jury

Kornelia Imesch Œchslin, professor, UNIL, Lausanne, Switzerland. Lecturer and jury

Amandine Oricheta, Association Le Cabanon, Lausanne, Switzerland. Jury

Verena Pierret, civil engineer, INGENI SA Lausanne, Switzerland. Technical expertise

Gérald Pilet, Sottas SA and SZS Stahlbau Zentrum Schweiz, Switzerland. Lecturer

Nikolai von Rosen, assistant, D-ARCH, ETH Zurich, Switzerland. Jury

Daniel Blaise Thorens, gallerist, Fine Art Gallery Basel, Switzerland. Lecturer

3 The Best Room

Marco De Michelis, professor, Università Iuav di Venezia, Italy. Lecturer

Marie Theres Stauffer, professor, Université de Genéve, Switzerland. Lecturer

III A Neuve Twin Pavilions

Tom Battin, professor, SBER-EPFL, Lausanne, Switzerland. Workshop

Pedro Machado Costa, architect, Machado Costa Arquitectos Associados, Portugal. Jury

Ulrich Delang, SAC CAS Club Alpine Suisse, Switzerland. Jury

Eik Frenzel, architect, Commission des Cabanes, Diablerets section, SAC CAS Club Alpine Suisse, Switzerland. Jury

Sven Fröhlich, architect, AFF Architekten, Berlin, Germany. Jury

Laboratory EAST   Partners

Martine Gabioud, warden of the A Neuve hut, SAC CAS Club Alpine Suisse, Switzerland. Jury

Julien Gamerro, doctoral student, iBOIS-EPFL, Lausanne, Switzerland. Jury and workshop

Sophia Haussener, professor, LRESE-EPFL, Lausanne, Switzerland. Workshop

Hendrik Huwald, professor, CRYOS-EPFL, Lausanne, Switzerland. Workshop

Marcel Isler, general secretary, Diablerets section, SAC CAS Club Alpine Suisse, Switzerland. Jury

Jean-François Kälin, civil engineer, Commission des Cabanes, Diablerets section, SAC CAS Club Alpine Suisse, Switzerland. Jury

Estelle Lepine, architect, LCC-EPFL, Lausanne, Switzerland. Lecturer

Götz Menzel, architect, GayMenzel, Monthey, Switzerland. Jury

Bertrand Merminod, professor, TOPO-EPFL, Lausanne, Switzerland. Workshop

Jean Micol, president, Diablerets section, SAC CAS Club Alpine Suisse, Switzerland. Jury

François Perrin, technical employee, iBOIS-EPFL, Lausanne, Switzerland. Technical expertise

Patrick Trösch, architect, Diablerets section, SAC CAS Club Alpine Suisse, Switzerland. Jury

4 Modern Times
Dieter Dietz, professor, ALICE-EPFL, Lausanne, Switzerland. Jury

Claudio Fetz, project manager, Migros Zurich, Switzerland. Jury

Dominique Ghiggi, landscape architect, Anton+Ghiggi Landschaft Architektur, Switzerland. Jury

Hermann Meier, real estate manager, Migros Zurich, Switzerland. Jury

Götz Menzel, architect, GayMenzel, Monthey, Switzerland. Jury

Jörg Rainer Noennig, professor, Laboratory of Knowledge Architecture, TU Dresden, Germany. Lecturer

Ruggero Tropeano, lecturer, Academy of Architecture USI, Mendrisio, Switzerland. Jury

5 Steal Schinkel
Stephanie Bender, architect, 2b Architects, Lausanne, Switzerland. Jury

Nicola Braghieri, professor, LAPIS-EPFL, Lausanne, Switzerland. Jury

Tobias Engelschall, architect, Descloux Engelschall Architekten, Germany. Jury

Etienne Descloux, architect, Descloux Engelschall Architekten, Germany. Jury

Corentin Fivet, professor, SXL-EPFL, Lausanne, Switzerland. Technical expertise and jury

Roland Fuhrmann, artist, Berlin, Germany. Jury

Christoph Gengnagel, professor, UdK, Berlin, Germany. Jury

Hilmar von Lojewski, urban planner, Association of German Cities, Berlin and Cologne, Germany. Jury

Karl-Heinz Schmitz, professor, Bauhaus-Universität Weimar, Germany. Jury

IV Traverse Art Pavilion
Francesca Bariviera, architect, UNI BAT, UNIL, Lausanne, Switzerland. Jury

Roger Boltshauser, architect, Boltshauser Architekten, Zurich, Switzerland. Jury

Karsten Födinger, artist, Berlin, Germany. Jury, design and production cooperation

Kornelia Imesch Öchslin, professor, UNIL, Lausanne, Switzerland. Jury

Steffen Marx, professor and civil engineer, Leibniz University Hannover, Germany. Jury

Friederike Meyer, architect and journalist for *Baunetz* and *Bauwelt*, Germany. Jury

Jean-Luc Mossier, directeur, PromFR, Etat de Fribourg, Switzerland Jury

Sonja Nagel, architect, Amunt Architekten, Stuttgart, Germany. Jury

Jean-Rodolphe Petter, Association Le Cabanon, Switzerland. Jury

Stanislas Rück, chef de service, SBC AKG, Etat de Fribourg, Switzerland. Jury

Laboratory EAST   Partners

Students

We would also like to thank all the students of the design studio EAST for their remarkable dedication and the high standards of their work.

A	Abdalla, Giovanni	pp. 408–19		Compain, Valentine	pp. 288–99, 367
	Antonuccio, Alyssa	p. 31		Comte, Adrien	p. 36
	Anfosso, Francesco	pp. 144–55, 309		Corthay, Emile	pp. 144, 318
	Allaz, Pauline	pp. 408–19		Crot, Julie	pp. 288–99, 371
	Ammeter, Emma	pp. 408–19	**D**	D'Antonio, Grégory	pp. 288–99, 375
B	Bagdjian, Lerna	pp. 144–55, 305		Dandan, Darine	pp. 288–99, 372
	Baldie, Amelia	pp. 144–55, 306		Darbellay, Léonard	pp. 12–23, 115, 176
	Baldy, Candice	pp. 12–23, 103, 164		Dayer, Charline	p. 39
	Balet, Lucas	pp. 408–19		De Benito Ortiz, Marta	pp. 288–99, 396
	Bardelloni, Marc	pp. 144–55, 310		De La Gandara, Marc	pp. 408–19
	Baudouin, Arnaud	p. 32		De Lima Carvalho, Ana	pp. 408–19
	Béguin, Antoine	pp. 12–23, 104, 167, 239		Déglon, Maya	pp. 144–55, 321
	Béris, Marie-Christine	pp. 144–55, 313		Delmuè, Raphael	pp. 288–99
	Bès, Amélie	pp. 408–19		Deville, Melchior	pp. 408–19
	Berney, Kimberley	pp. 288–99, 363		Dias, Elodie	pp. 288–99, 368
	Ben Hallam, Houssam	pp. 288–99, 375		Di Martino, Clea	pp. 408–19
	Bianchi, Francesca	pp. 288–99, 364		Din, Charlotte	pp. 144–55, 321
	Bianchi, Vincent	pp. 288–99		Di Rosa, Sophie	pp. 12–23, 116, 179, 247
	Bichelmeier, Ian	pp. 144–55, 314		Disner, Gabriel	pp. 12–23, 119, 180, 248
	Biétry, Marlon	pp. 12–23, 107, 168, 240		Dolci, Noemi	pp. 144–55, 322
	Bionda, Giancarlo	pp. 408–19		Dubois, Florent	pp. 288–99, 379
	Bodevin, Victoria	pp. 12–23, 108		Ducommun, Emilien	pp. 288–99, 376
	Bollschweiler, Robin	pp. 144–55, 313	**E**	El Hayek, Christopher	pp. 12–23, 120, 183, 251
	Borchardt, Alicia	pp. 144–55, 317		El Karmoudi, Yasmine	pp. 288–99, 388
	Bornet, Laura	pp. 144–55, 309		Endres, Karoline	pp. 144–55, 325
	Bosman, Axelle	pp. 408–19		Escallier, Pénélope	pp. 288–99
C	Cantale, Laure	p. 35		Esteves Lopes, Helena	p. 48
	Caspary, Félix	pp. 12–23, 111, 171		Evéquoz, Marc	pp. 12–23, 123, 184, 252
	Chareton, Gabriel	pp. 12–23, 112, 172	**F**	Fahrni, Sarah-Kristina	p. 40
	Chizzolini, Enrico	pp. 288–99, 368		Fardel, Michèle	pp. 144–55, 326
	Choukroun, Anne	pp. 144–55, 306		Farra, Sami	pp. 12–23, 115, 187, 255
	Claessens, Yannick	pp. 12–23, 175, 243		Faure, Aude	pp. 288–99, 380

	Fellrath, Silouane	pp. 144–55, 310
	Fol, Floriane	pp. 144–55, 314
	Fonjallaz, Marion	pp. 408–19
G	Gandor, Anne-Claire	pp. 288–99, 383
	Gauchoux, Léa	pp. 12–23, 111, 188, 256
	Gmür, Benjamin	p. 43
	Gobet, Thomas	pp. 408–19
	Goolaub, Nila	pp. 144–55, 329
	Grossrieder, Aline	p. 44
H	Helfenstein, Mathias	pp. 408–19
	Henkel, Julius	p. 47
	Hersche, Viviane	pp. 408–19
	Huegi, Quentin	pp. 288–99, 383
I	Imadiouni, Omar	pp. 288–99, 384
	Inhelder, Jonas	pp. 144–55, 318
	Ishii, Andrea	pp. 288–99, 363
J	Jaccard, Samuel	pp. 288–99
	Jancu, Juliette	pp. 12–23, 124, 191, 259
	Jaques, Valentine	pp. 288–99, 387
	Jenny, Charles	pp. 12–23, 127, 192, 260
	Joly-Pottuz, Chloe	pp. 12–23, 128, 195
	Jost, Jessica	pp. 408–19
K	Kadrijaj, Gentian	pp. 12–23, 127, 196, 263
	Karpushov, Alexander	pp. 12–23, 131, 199
L	Lai, Mélanie	pp. 144–55, 326
	Läng, Thomas	pp. 408–19
	Legrain, Théophile	pp. 12–23, 112, 200, 264
	Liaudat, Adrien	pp. 144–55, 305
	Liebich, Alexandra	pp. 12–23, 132, 203
	Li, Siying	pp. 288–99, 380
	Lopes, Daniela	pp. 288–99, 379
	Louhichi, Younes	pp. 288–99, 391
	Lurati, Elena	p. 51
	Lutz, Thomas	pp. 144–55, 330
M	Mahfouz, Amira	p. 52
	Maloukotsi, Afroditi	pp. 12–23, 124, 204, 267
	Merz, Basil	pp. 408–19
	Meuwly, Adrien	p. 55
	Miguet, Arnaud	pp. 288–99, 395
	Morris, Jeremy	pp. 408–19
	Mosca, Nina	pp. 144–55, 333
	Moutal, Marion	pp. 288–99, 388
	Morris, Jeremy	pp. 408–19
	Muller, Adrien	p. 56
N	Nahmani, Julia	p. 60
	Nebel, Pierre	p. 59
	Nyffeler, Florence	pp. 288–99, 387
O	Ortelli, Alessandra	pp. 408–19
P	Paragon, Camille	pp. 144–55, 325
	Parpoil, Felix	p. 63
	Patarot, Alessandra	p. 64
	Perret, David	pp. 408–19
	Péquignot, Laure	pp. 12–23, 207
	Pham, Tim	pp. 12–23, 119
	Pittet, Christophe	pp. 67, 288–99
	Prins, Charlotte	p. 68
	Prongué, Jérémy	pp. 288–99, 364
R	Rapin, Matthieu	pp. 144–55, 330
	Rausis, Justine	pp. 12–23, 128, 208, 268
	Rey, Valentin	pp. 12–23, 104, 211
	Reymond, Joane	p. 71
	Reymond, Marc	pp. 12–23, 116, 212
	Richard, Soukaïna	pp. 288–99, 372
	Richner, David	pp. 12–23, 123, 215, 271
	Roche-Meredith, Charl.	pp. 288–99, 392
	Rodrigues, Pascal	pp. 144–55, 329
	Routhier, Séverine	pp. 288–99, 396
	Roy, Lucien	pp. 408–19
	Rozenberg, Merlin	pp. 408–19
	Ruiz, Margaux	pp. 12–23, 108, 216, 272
	Rychner, Nicolas	pp. 288–99, 371
	Rydenvald, Noël	pp. 288–99
S	Saby, Franceline	pp. 144–55
	Sadek, Maryem	pp. 288–99, 399
	Sartorio, Sébastien	p. 72
	Savoy, Anne-Michèle	pp. 144–55, 321
	Senn, Eda	pp. 408–19
	Sivunen, Salla	pp. 288–99, 399
	Soulier, Laurent	pp. 288–99, 400
	Spagnoli, Djuna	pp. 144–55, 317
	Steinfels, Constance	pp. 288–99, 367
	Stierli, Diane	pp. 12–23, 135, 219, 275
	Stoll, Laura	pp. 12–23, 136, 220
	Studer, Bastardo	p. 76
	Suris, Bertran	p. 75
T	Takhtravanchi, Maseeh	pp. 288–99, 376
	Thévenoz, Loris	pp. 144–55, 333
	Thiébaud, Romain	pp. 12–23, 103, 223, 276
U	Uka, Fiona	pp. 144–55, 322
	Uldry, Sabine	pp. 144–55, 334
V	Valla, Bénédicte	pp. 144–55, 334
	Van, Andrea	pp. 288–99, 395
	Varone, Alexane	pp. 408–19
	Vennemann, Xenia	p. 79
	Vertesi, Marc	pp. 12–23, 107, 224
	Vexina Wilkinson, Teo	pp. 12–23, 120, 227, 279
	Vieillecroze, Charles	p. 80
	Viennet, Mathieu	pp. 288–99
	Voutat, Maude	pp. 408–19
W	Wahlen, Henri	pp. 144–55, 310
	Widmann, Julia	p. 83
	Worreth, Killian	pp. 12–23, 131, 228, 280
	Wyssbrod, Marine	pp. 12–23, 135, 231, 283
Z	Ziörjen, Ursina	pp. 12–23, 136, 232
	Zong, Chujun	p. 384
	Zurbriggen, Noémie	pp. 408–19

Colophon

École Polytechnique
Fédérale de Lausanne (EPFL)

School of Architecture,
Civil and Environmental
Engineering (ENAC)

Institute of Architecture (IA)

Laboratory of Elementary
Architecture and Studies of
Types (EAST)

EAST Directors
Prof. Martin Fröhlich
Prof. Dr Anja Fröhlich

Team, 2013–2018
Giulia Altarelli
Tiago P. Borges
Antje Bittorf
Maxence Derlet
Sebastian F. Lippok
Sophie Shiraishi

Student assistants
Alyssa Antonuccio
Yannick Claessens
Christopher El Hayek
Daniela Lopes Peñaloza
Charlotte Prins
Valentino Vitacca
Marine Wyssbrod

Copy editing
Thomas Skelton-Robinson

Translations
Julian Reisenberger

Proofreading
Ian McDonald

Design
Ivo Wojcik (ivo-wojcik.com)

**Lithography, printing
and binding**
DZA Druckerei zu Altenburg
GmbH, Thüringen

Copyright
© 2019 Laboratory EAST,
École Polytechnique
Fédérale de Lausanne and
Park Books AG, Zurich

The copyright of all texts
lies with the respective
author(s).

The copyright of images
lies with the respective
originator(s) or subsequent
copyright owner(s).

Image credits: p. 431

Park Books
Niederdorfstrasse 54
8001 Zürich
Switzerland
www.park-books.com

Park Books is being supported by the Federal Office of Culture with a general subsidy for the years 2016–2020.

All rights reserved; no part of this publication may be reproduced, stored in a retrieval system or transmitted in any form or by any means, electronic, mechanical, photocopying, recording, or otherwise, without the prior written consent of the publisher.

If possible, the authors, editor and publisher have attempted to ascertain the authors, originators and owners of all copyrighted material. In the case of errors or omissions, please inform us and we shall rectify any necessary details in subsequent editions of this book.

ISBN 978-3-03860-138-8

Image Credits

Every reasonable attempt has been made by the authors, editors and publishers to identify the owners of copyrights. Errors and omissions will be corrected in subsequent editions. p. 8 Alyssa Antonuccio (left), Joel Tettamanti (top right), Christophe El Hayek & Teo Vexina Wilkinson (bottom right); p. 9 Sebastian Lippok (top right), Félix Louis Caspary (top left), Christophe El Hayek (bottom left), Joel Tettamanti (bottom right); p. 10 Anne-Claire Gandor & Quentin Huegi (top left), Darine Dandan & Soukaïna Richard (top right), Karsten Födinger (bottom); p. 24 Benjamin Gmür (top), Julia Nahmani; p. 25 Pierre Nebel; p. 92 Courtesy of Rob Krier (top); p. 93 Karl Friedrich Schinkel, Collection of architectural designs: containing partly works which are executed, partly objects whose execution was intended (Berlin: Ernst & Korn, 1858) ETH-Bibliothek Zürich, Rar 9822, http://doi.org/10.3931/e-rara-9013 Public Domain Mark (left), ©Eredi Aldo Rossi, courtesy of Fondazione Aldo Rossi (right); p. 94 Schneider-Wessling (bottom); p. 95 Courtesy of James Wines, SITE Group; p. 97 Courtesy of Yona Friedman (top and bottom right); p. 98 Christophe El Hayek & Teo Wilkinson; p. 99 Marc Evéquoz & David Richner; p. 140 Reprinted from Joseph Fenton, Lynnette Widder and Kenneth Kaplan, "Hybrid Buildings" in Livio Dimitriu (ed.) *Pamphlet Architecture 1–10*. Vol. 1–10 (New York: Princeton Architectural Press, 1998), p.11; p. 141 Reprinted from Ibid., pp.16–17 and pp.26–27; p. 142 Reprinted from catalogue *Buildings for Best Products*, The Museum of Modern Art (New York: The Museum of Modern Art MoMA, 1979), pp. 22–23 (top), Ibid. p. 25 (bottom); p. 143 Illustrations reprinted from Ibid., p.25 ; p. 156 Félix Louis Caspary; p. 157 Sami Farra; p. 259 John Miller; p. 286 [Fig.1] Reprinted from Eugène Viollet-le-Duc, *Dictionnaire raisonné de l'architecture française du XIe au XVIe siècle*, Vol. 6 (Paris: Bance-Morel, 1863), p. 286. München, Bayerische Staatsbibliothek, 4 A.civ. 84 nb-6, http://www.mdz-nbn-resolving.de/urn/resolver.pl?urn=urn:nbn:de:bvb:12-bsb10048549-8 / Public Domain Mark (Out of copyright – non commercial re-use), [Fig.2] Reprinted from Wolfram Prinz, *Das französische Schloss der Renaissance. Form und Bedeutung der Architektur, ihre geschichtlichen und gesellschaftlichen Grundlagen.* (Berlin: Mann, 1985), p.535, [Fig.3] Reprinted from Charles Augustin d'Aviler, *Cours d'architecture, qui comprend les ordres de Vignole.* (Paris: Langlois, 1691), p.176. ETH-Bibliothek Zürich, RAR 457, http://doi.org/10.3931/e-rara-90 / Public Domain Mark.; p. 287 [Fig.5] Reprinted from Jaques-François Blondel, *Architecture Françoise, ou Recueil des Plans, Elevations, Coupes et Profils des Eglises, Maisons Royales, Palais, Hôtel & Edifices les plus considérables [...] : avec la description de ces Edifices, & des dissertations utiles & intéressantes sur chaque espece de Bâtiment : Une Introduction à l'Architecture, un Abrégé Historique de la Ville de Paris, & la description des principaux Edifices du Faubourg St.Germain*, Bd. I (Paris: Jombert, 1752), after p.220. ETH-Bibliothek Zürich, Rar 965: 1 GF, http://doi.org/10.3931/e-rara-9340 / Public Domain Mark, [Fig.6] Arvind J. Talati ©FLC / 2019, ProLitteris, Zurich; p. 300 Marie-Christine Béris & Robin Bollschweiler; p. 301 Noemi Dolci & Fiona Uka; pp. 346–7 [Fig.1–6] Reprinted from *Perspecta*, 12, 1969; p. 348 [Fig.7] Reprinted from Werner Blaser, *Mies van der Rohe* (Zurich: Verlag für Architektur, 1965) Courtesy of Werner Blaser (top), [Fig.8] Reprinted from Le Corbusier and Pierre Jeanneret, *Œuvre Comtplete 1910–1929* (Zurich: Les Editions d'Architecture, Erlenbach, 1946) (bottom); p. 349 [Fig.9–10] Reprinted from Alexander Klein, *Das Einfamilienhaus* (Stuttgart: Julius Hoffman Verlag, 1934); p. 350 [Fig.11] Courtesy of Leon Krier, [Fig.12] *Learning from Las Vegas*, by Robert Venturi, Denise Scott Brown and Steven Izenour, reprinted courtesy of the MIT Press; p. 351 [Fig.13] Ibid.; [Fig.14–15] Courtesy of Rafael Moneo; p. 356 Valentine Compain & Constance Steinfels; p. 357 Anne-Claire Gandor, Questin Huegi; p. 406 Reprinted from Karl Friedrich Schinkel, *Collection of Architectural Designs: Including Designs Which Have Been Executed and Objects Whose Execution Was Intended.* New Complete Ed. in CLXXIV Plates, [facsimile Ed.] ed. (New York: Princeton Architectural Press, 1989) (bottom left / right), Reprinted from Tilmann Buddensieg, "'Bauen wie man wolle…' Schinkels Vorstellungen von der Baufreiheit", in *Daidalos*, 7 (1983) (middle), Reprinted from Tilmann Buddensieg, "Bildungsstadt und Arbeitsstadt – Schinkels Berliner Stadtbaukunst und das 20. Jahrhundert", in Hans Kollhoff & Fritz Neumeyer (eds.) *Grosstadtarchitektur* (Berlin: 1989) (top); p. 407 Karl Friedrich Schinkel, Ibid.

ISBN 978-3-0386O-138-8